✔ How to Pass

SECOND EDITION

HIGHER

Business Management

Craig McLeod

HODDER
GIBSON
AN HACHETTE UK COMPANY

Dedication

I would like to thank the following people for their help, either directly or indirectly, in writing this book:

Hugh Donnelly, Director at Co-operative Education Trust Scotland for his input into the democratic enterprises text.

Kieron Gallagher, Head of Governance at SEPA, for his assistance and guidance with the SEPA case study and other topics in this book.

Rhona Sivewright, Principal Assessor of Higher Business Management, and the rest of the Higher team for their years of guidance and support through my various roles in the SQA.

Jim Morrison, Senior Team Leader for Higher BM and Faculty Head at Lowden Academy, for his assistance with the SEPA case study.

My faculty in Auchmuty High School for their support, friendship and leading the sector in reminding us all why teaching is a truly noble profession and super job – most of the time!

At Hodder Gibson, Claire Spinks and Kirsty Taylor for making everything run so smoothly. Charlotte Hiorns and Nicola MacGregor for being a huge help with this edition.

Last, but by no means least, my wife Debbie for endless hours of proofreading, moral support and putting up with me spending hours at the laptop while being the most super mum to our wee boy!

The Publishers would like to thank the following for permission to reproduce copyright material:

Photo credits

p.4 © Subway; **p.8** Jamie Oliver's Fifteen, Photo © David Loftus; **p.9** © The Co-operative Group; **p.12** © Lush Digital; **p.16** © Google Inc; **p.17** © Procter & Gamble; **p.19** © Marvel/Disney/Kobal/REX/Shutterstock; **p.23** © Findlay / Alamy Stock Photo; **p.33** © ROBYN BECK/ AFP/Getty Images; **p.34** top © TBC/Shutterstock; bottom © innocent Drinks; **p.50** © AVAVA – Fotolia.com; **p.61** © Nestlé; **p.68** © A.P.S. (UK) / Alamy Stock Photo; **p.70** top © Tesco PLC; bottom © J Sainsbury plc; **p.72** © Susie Slatter / Alamy Stock Photo; **p.73** © Realimage /Alamy Stock Photo; **p.75** © Laura De Meo/Shutterstock; **p.77** © Universal/Kobal/REX/Shutterstock; **p.80** © Tom Gowanlock / Alamy Stock Photo; **p.89** © Justin Kaseztwoz / Alamy Stock Photo; **p.90** © Small Town Studio – Fotolia.com; **p.91** © Betsie Van der Meer/Stone/ Getty Images; **p.92** © Everett Collection Historical / Alamy; **p.95** © BSI; **p.97** © Cruelty Free International; **p.99** © Steven May / Alamy Stock Photo; **p.118** top © Unison; bottom © Unite the Union.

Acknowledgements

SQA Outcomes and Assessment Standards adapted by the author and used with permission – copyright © Scottish Qualifications Authority. Unless otherwise specified, data used in the creation of graphics throughout this book is public domain.

Every effort has been made to trace all copyright holders, but if any have been inadvertently overlooked, the Publishers will be pleased to make the necessary arrangements at the first opportunity.

Although every effort has been made to ensure that website addresses are correct at time of going to press, Hodder Gibson cannot be held responsible for the content of any website mentioned in this book. It is sometimes possible to find a relocated web page by typing in the address of the home page for a website in the URL window of your browser.

Hachette UK's policy is to use papers that are natural, renewable and recyclable products and made from wood grown in well-managed forests and other controlled sources. The logging and manufacturing processes are expected to conform to the environmental regulations of the country of origin.

Orders: please contact Bookpoint Ltd, 130 Park Drive, Milton Park, Abingdon, Oxon OX14 4SE. Telephone: (44) 01235 827827. Fax: (44) 01235 400454. Email education@bookpoint.co.uk Lines are open from 9 a.m. to 5 p.m., Monday to Saturday, with a 24-hour message answering service. Visit our website at www.hoddereducation.co.uk. If you have queries or questions that aren't about an order, you can contact us at hoddergibson@hodder.co.uk

© Craig McLeod 2019

First published in 2019 by
Hodder Gibson, an imprint of Hodder Education
An Hachette UK Company
211 St Vincent Street
Glasgow, G2 5QY

Impression number   5 4 3
Year   2023 2022 2021 2020 2019

SCOTLAND EXCEL
We are an approved supplier on the Scotland Excel framework.
Schools can find us on their procurement system as:
Hodder & Stoughton Limited t/a Hodder Gibson.

Cover photo © jannoon028 - stock.adobe.com
Illustrations by Barking Dog Art Design and Illustration
Typeset in Cronos Pro Light 13/15pt by Aptara, Inc.
Printed in India
A catalogue record for this title is available from the British Library.
ISBN: 978 1 5104 5239 8

MIX
Paper from responsible sources
FSC
www.fsc.org   FSC™ C104740

Contents

Introduction

Welcome to *How to Pass Higher Business Management*. This book has been written specifically to prepare you for the new Higher Business Management course. It will help you pass the coursework assignment and question paper set by the Scottish Qualifications Authority (SQA). However, that doesn't mean you have to *learn* everything in this book or indeed that this book contains *everything* you could possibly need to know in an assessment situation. If you haven't realised already, Higher Business Management is a dynamic (this means always changing) course that is relevant to real life. In other words, there are endless possibilities when it comes to answering questions that can be exemplified by your own experiences of business as well as what you study in this book. You can also follow the author of this book on Twitter **@mrmcleodbized** for daily Higher Business Management hints and tips in the lead up to exams!

The subject

What do you mean, you have no experience of business? Of course you do! Every time you go into a shop, watch a TV advert or surf the internet for new clothes, you are engaging with *business*. Perhaps you have a part-time job or have taken part in work experience at school? These experiences will stand you in good stead when studying Higher Business Management.

Higher Business Management has grown in popularity over recent years. Many students like it for the reasons outlined above, that is, it is relevant to real life and interesting enough to pass the time with at school. Another reason why it is so popular, especially with those students 'crashing' the subject (that is attempting the Higher without having studied National 5), is because the course assumes no previous knowledge. There are some subjects that you have been studying since you were five. Sometimes it is difficult to attempt a Higher in something you have found tough throughout your school life. Well, the great thing about Business Management is that because the subject material is constantly being updated and is taught from scratch by your teacher each year, everyone starts at the same point, engaging with content that is relevant to them. As long as you are hard-working, revisit the day's lesson at home each night and listen to your teacher's advice, you will pass the course! Oh, and make sure you endeavour to write in proper sentences, too!

How to use this book

The book contains a number of features that are designed to help you make the most of your studies. They are:

What you should know

These highlight key learning outcomes that you *must* know in order to demonstrate enough knowledge to meet the **assessment standards** for each section, as set by the SQA. Your teacher can, and will, assess you in a variety of ways, for example written tests, presentations, reports and so on. However, in all assessments you must prove that you meet these standards.

Hints & tips

This feature gives you examiners' hints and tips on how to achieve top marks. It also highlights common mistakes to watch out for and avoid!

Remember

This feature provides examiners' advice on what key terms to remember, and how. It also suggests what you need to do to gain the maximum marks available in your final course assessment.

WWW

Useful up-to-date weblinks to help bring the topics to life for you.

Case study

These present real-life examples of business, with points for discussion to deepen your understanding of key topics.

Activity

Hands-on tasks that will help you revise each topic.

Quick questions

Short-answer questions to help you digest the information in each assessment standard.

Key questions

These are questions you must prove you can answer to meet the assessment standard and pass each outcome if you wish to pass the level 6 unit.

Exam-style questions practice

These questions are written in the style of the external question-paper questions, complete with fully worked solutions, and hints and tips at the back of the book to help you prepare for your exam.

The course

The Higher Business Management course is split into five areas of study:

- 1: Understanding business
- 2: Management of marketing
- 3: Management of operations
- 4: Management of people
- 5: Management of finance

Each chapter is divided into topics which cover the knowledge and understanding, and the mandatory skills required for each area.

Course assessment

The course assessment for Higher Business Management is made up of two components:

1 Question paper (90 marks, 75% of overall grade).
2 Coursework assignment (30 marks, 25% of overall grade).

Question paper

The **question paper** is set by the SQA and will be taken during the main examination diet. The exam is *closed book*, so you won't have access to notes or books.

The question paper is designed to give you the opportunity to apply your knowledge and understanding of business concepts from all topics in the course. This is your chance to show the examiner what you are made of! You should be ready for this, even excited to get in there and have the chance to pull together a year of studying to get the grade you deserve!

The question paper has two sections:

Section 1 (30 marks): This is known as a 'case study' and will be made up of a main case study text with *exhibits* containing additional information. This section will consist of *mandatory* short answer questions (that is you must answer *all* of them), each worth between 1 and 8 marks, based on the case study.

Remember

Questions will require you to *demonstrate* your skills, knowledge and understanding from studying the course *AND* your ability to *apply* them to the case study. In other words, all the answers are not contained in the case study and exhibits provided – you will need to draw on relevant material from your studies. There will be 0 marks for **lifting** information word for word from the case study and writing it as your answer. Likewise, you will not get full marks if you just regurgitate knowledge from your studies without applying it to the context of the case study and questions.

> **Hints & tips** ★
>
> Try the exam-style case study at the back of this book to get practice at this key exam skill and make sure to check the solution and hints and tips too!

Section 2 (60 marks): This section will consist of four 15-mark questions based on the following areas: Understanding business, Management of marketing, Management of operations, Management of people or Management of finance. These questions are your chance for big marks, you don't have to worry about linking with a case study – just go for it and show the examiner what you have learned!

Command words

Command words are used in each question in the question paper. The command word is usually the first word of the question and is designed to guide you to answer the question in the way in which it is intended to be answered.

Below is a list of the *common* command words used in Higher Business Management questions with advice on how you should tackle them. Further hints and tips on how to interpret command words can be found in the Solutions to exam-style questions section at the end of this book.

> **Hints & tips** ★
>
> Yes, some Section 2 questions can be daunting as they can be up to 8 marks and cover ANY topic from the course. But don't leave ANY answer blank! Write something and you just never know!

Command word	Explanation	Hints and tips
Identify	Present in brief form.	Simply name or state. No detailed description is required.
Outline	Provide a brief summary of content.	More than identifying, but not a detailed description.
Describe	Make a number of relevant factual points, e.g. characteristics and/or features.	Write descriptions in full sentences. These are more than just 'outlines' of facts.
Discuss	Communicate issues, ideas or information that make a case for and/or against.	Describe advantages/disadvantages, costs/benefits, etc. Use the link word 'however' to flip between costs/benefits, advantages/disadvantages. Please note that you don't always have to give both sides of the debate.
Compare	Demonstrate knowledge and understanding of the similarities and/or differences between two things, methods, features or choices.	Use the link word 'both' to illustrate similarities between two things and 'whereas' to illustrate differences. The points of comparison must be *related*, i.e. not just two random points.
Distinguish	Demonstrate knowledge and understanding of the differences between methods, features or choices.	Treat this question in a similar way to 'Compare' questions. However, *only* differences should be given, i.e. only use 'whereas' to illustrate differences in 'Distinguish' questions.
Justify	Give reasons to support suggestions or courses of action.	Giving a justification is basically like describing an *advantage* of doing something. Don't ever give a *disadvantage* as this isn't justifying.
Explain	Make points that relate cause and effect and/or make the relationships clear.	You can treat answering these questions as making two statements for 1 mark. To gain each mark you need to relate *cause* and *effect*. There are two ways you can do this: 1) Use the link phrases 'this means', 'meaning' and 'which will' to explain the *effect* after giving a *cause*. 2) Use the link phrase 'as' or 'because' to explain the *cause* after giving the *effect* first.

Exam questions

You should practise exam questions containing all of the command words on page viii. A good way to understand the differences between the command words is to tackle similar questions but with different command words. You will be able to see the differences in the content and quantity of writing needed to gain marks for each one.

You will be able to find similar questions with different command words on the SQA website, www.sqa.org.uk. There they have guidance on which questions you can use from the *old* Higher as well as specimen questions from the *new* Higher. There are also exam-style questions at the end of each chapter in this book. You can also study the solutions provided to see how they should be tackled – after attempting them, of course!

You also need to be aware of the wording of each question as this can give you clues about how to answer it. Let's break down an example question to see what it tells us.

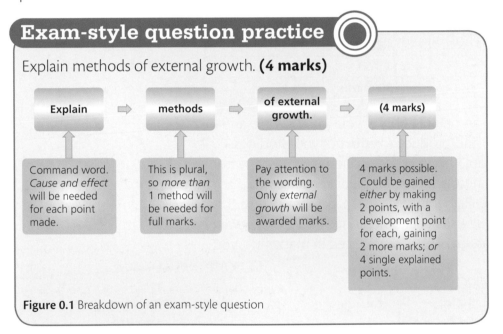

Exam-style question practice

Explain methods of external growth. **(4 marks)**

Explain	methods	of external growth.	(4 marks)
Command word. *Cause and effect* will be needed for each point made.	This is plural, so *more than* 1 method will be needed for full marks.	Pay attention to the wording. Only *external growth* will be awarded marks.	4 marks possible. Could be gained *either* by making 2 points, with a development point for each, gaining 2 more marks; *or* 4 single explained points.

Figure 0.1 Breakdown of an exam-style question

Activity 0.1

Below are five exam-style questions, all on the same straightforward 'introductory' topic that you should cover in the early stages of the course. Attempt all five questions, paying close attention to the command word in each one. Check your answers with a partner or ask your teacher to look over them for you.

1 Describe the features of:
   a) a private limited company
   b) a public limited company. **(4 marks)**
2 Discuss the following types of organisation:
   a) a private limited company
   b) a public limited company. **(4 marks)**
3 Compare the following types of organisation:
   a private limited company and a public limited company. **(4 marks)**
   ⇨

4 Distinguish between the following types of organisation: a private limited company and a public limited company. **(4 marks)**

5 Explain why a business would want to:
   a) become a public limited company
   b) remain a private limited company. **(4 marks)**

Coursework assignment

The **coursework assignment** is worth 30 marks (25% of your overall grade) and will be completed by you at school or college and sent to the SQA to be marked. The marks will be awarded as follows:

Element	Maximum marks available
Introduction	2 marks
Research	4 marks
Analysis and interpretation	13 marks
Conclusions and recommendations	10 marks
Collating and reporting findings	1 mark
Total	**30 marks**

Your assignment is to research an organisation of your choice AND a **business issue** of your choice, and produce a **report** of your findings. The organisation can be from any sector of the economy, that is, private, public or third sector. The business issue should be directly related to a topic and/or concept from the Higher Business Management course. This should not be an entire area but a specific topic. For example if you want to investigate Coca-Cola and are particularly interested in marketing, you could choose:
- the pricing strategies of Coca-Cola
- the product portfolio of Coca-Cola
- the extended marketing mix of Coca-Cola
- the out-of-the-pipeline promotions of Coca-Cola.

Once you have decided on your organisation and business issue, you then have to plan and gather evidence as well as typing up your report. You have 8 hours to do this. Make sure you split the time up appropriately – don't spend too long researching background information on your chosen organisation for the introduction as this section is only worth 2 marks.

Let's take a look at each section.

Introduction (2 marks)

The **introduction** should set the tone of your report.
1 First, you *must* state the organisation you are researching and the business issue you have chosen.
2 Second, you *must* state the topic you have chosen.
3 You should give some background information on the organisation, for example, a brief history, the product or service it provides, their

target market, the structure of the organisation, and so on. Limit this information to two points only but **make sure** you describe what the business does, i.e. what it makes/sells/provides.

Research (4 marks)

The **research** section requires you to justify the methods of research you have chosen.

1 You must choose at least two sources of information. These can be gathered via field or desk research. For example:
   - websites – your chosen business and/or the competition's
   - review sites – a quick way to access customer opinions
   - social media – you may have to gather this evidence at home
   - surveys – you could set up an online survey to ask your classmates questions
   - personal interviews – perhaps with a customer or an employee if you can
   - notes from field trips or guest speakers
   - newspapers/magazines/catalogues – can provide valuable visual evidence.
2 You have to explain why you have chosen these sources – what was the **purpose** of each source, what do you hope to find out?
3 You should also explain the value of each source, for example, the advantages of using the source.
4 *Do not* list everything you found out from your research in this section; this is done later.

Remember

This is the analysis section – don't offer any recommendations yet as you will receive no marks!

Analysis and interpretation (13 marks)

The **analysis and interpretation** section is the main body of your report where you present your findings from your research.

Each analysis and interpretation point you make should relate to evidence from your research. This evidence could be presented as a graph, image or table and can be included as an appendix at the end of your report, signposted in this section. For example, Source 1, Source 2, and so on.

1 Your research evidence could also be analysed using an **analytical technique**. Examples of analytical techniques you could use are:
   - Marketing mix analysis
   - SWOT analysis
   - PESTEC analysis
   - product portfolio (Boston matrix)
   - ratio analysis
2 Each point you make should be analysed. You can either suggest reasons for the finding or explain impacts of the finding on the business.
   In other words *don't* just list your research evidence; you must *add* to each piece of evidence and show the marker you have analysed EACH finding.

Hints & tips

A good way to ensure you **analyse** your research evidence is to reference or write out a piece of evidence and then write 'this shows...' or 'it is clear that...' before analysing what it shows or tells you in relation to your topic!

Conclusions and recommendations (10 marks)

This is the final section of your report, woo hoo!

1 You should make **conclusions** based on positives that you have found, so explain the likely benefits of something the organisation does well, based on your evidence.

2 You should also make **recommendations** based on negatives that you have found, so explain what the organisation should change, introduce or do better *and* the benefits and costs of doing so.

Collating and reporting (1 mark)

You don't have to do anything specific in this section, just ensure that:

● you have used appropriate headings throughout the report

● your report isn't too long: 2,000 words (+/− 10%)

● you have used appropriate display materials, for example, charts, graphs, images

● you have used business terminology throughout the report.

Revision tips

There are three things you must do to prepare for the Higher Business Management exam. They are: revise, revise and revise! Sure, a lot of Business Management is common sense and you can write about experiences you have of business. However, the course has its fair share of topics that you won't know before you study the course and won't remember your teacher teaching you either. So, you *have* to revise.

Here are a few things you can do to make your revision effective.

Key terms spreadsheet

Creating and updating a key terms spreadsheet should be an ongoing revision activity that you do throughout your studies. If it is already too late, try creating one during your study leave as you revise each topic.

Activity 0.2

1 Create a table using spreadsheet software, add four columns: Term, Definition, Advantage and Disadvantage.

2 Use the Glossary at the back of this book to find out what key terms are used in the course and so should be on your list. Try and pick out the ones you know first and define them yourself. Then look up the terms you don't know or can't remember.

3 Revise these terms. Copy down some notes, use the internet to find out some more and then update your spreadsheet. You can sort your spreadsheet alphabetically or you could have a different sheet for each topic. It's up to you.

Hints & tips

Many candidates struggle with this section:

✓ When concluding, don't re-word your findings (no marks); try to 'sum up' the analysis.

✓ Justify your recommendations, i.e. refer back to findings and say WHY the business should follow your advice.

✓ Develop your recommendations by explaining possible impacts on the business.

Hints & tips

Make sure you are awarded the mark for 'collating and reporting', e.g. it is recommended that you use 11pt font size with 1.5 line spacing and include page numbers. You should view this as a free mark that will only be lost through lack of care and attention on your part!

Questions that give you the fear!

As you revise by tackling exam-style questions – either from this book, the SQA website or from your teacher – there will be questions that you really don't like the look of. In other words, they give you 'the fear'! A revision technique I use with my own students at school is to stop avoiding these questions and actually *embrace* them. You should do this too! The more you practise answering them, the more straightforward and less daunting they will become.

So, flick through the exam-style questions in this book, specimen papers, old past papers, and so on and make a list of the questions for which, off the top of your head, you can't think of an answer that would score you *at least half* of the available marks. These are your 'fear' questions. Don't avoid them; revise them. (Chances are the extra time you spend looking at these areas will be all it takes to give you some confidence.) Attempt the question. Don't worry if you can't get full marks; remember, you *were* struggling to get even some or any marks before! Take your answer to your teacher or check it yourself.

It is also especially important to do this, as all questions in the final exam are mandatory so, you never know – the type of questions that give you the fear might just come up!

Mind maps

Mind maps are useful in Higher Business Management as there is so much jargon, theory and terms.

- Ever heard the phrase 'a picture is worth a thousand words'? Including visual representations of the information, as drawings and images, in your revision notes will really help it stick in your mind.
- What is more, by the time you finish the course, you should start to see patterns emerging and the same theory being repeated in different topics – and this will be easy to see when you compare your mind maps.
- You can make a mind map on paper or on a computer – a number of kinds of free mind mapping software are available.
- Try making a mind map with a friend. One of you can even record the other drawing your mind map (perhaps after a few practice shots!) and, when you speed it up, it will make a neat revision video. You could even dub commentary over the top.

Make sure you go into that exam ready for it. As an examiner myself, I know when a candidate is prepared – it leaps right off the page when I mark their question paper. Make sure that's how your question paper looks!

Enjoy the course, enjoy your studies and all the very best.

Now, on with the book!

> **Hints & tips**
>
> There are a number of diagrams/charts in this course. Revise these and add to your revision notes/mind maps. They are often easier to remember than large areas of text and can be worth marks in the exam.

> **Remember**
>
> ... passing Higher Business Management is down to *you* – your hard work, *your* revision, *you* paying attention in class. You have to submit the best assignment *you* possibly can and make sure *you* answer every question in the exam to the best of *your* ability – never leave a question blank! But *you* can do it – there is nothing stopping *you*!

Chapter 1 Understanding business

Role of business in society

What you should know

- ★ How business activity adds value
- ★ How business activity satisfies needs and wants
- ★ Sectors of industry
- ★ Sectors of the economy

Why do businesses exist?

Businesses exist primarily to satisfy the **needs** and **wants** of customers.
- Needs are essential to survive, e.g. food, water, shelter and toilets.
- Wants are *everything* else, e.g. designer clothing, transport, holidays and even Wi-Fi and smartphones!

Often people will say, 'I *need* my phone' or 'Phew, I *need* a holiday', but these items aren't essential for humans to live so they are not needs.

Remember

... the difference between **goods** and **services**! Goods are things that you buy that are tangible (you can physically touch them). A service is something you use. They are intangible (you can't physically see or touch them). Both goods and services are known as **products**.

Sectors of industry

At Higher level Business Management, you need to be aware of **four** sectors of industry:

1. **Primary sector**. This consists of businesses that are involved in exploiting natural resources. Examples include farming, mining and oil drilling.
2. **Secondary sector**. This consists of businesses that are involved in manufacturing and construction, by taking natural resources and turning them into **goods** that can be sold later. Examples include electronics manufacture, car production and house building.
3. **Tertiary sector**. This consists of businesses and organisations that are involved in providing **services** rather than goods. Examples include retail outlets, banks, hotels and hospitals.
4. **Quaternary sector**. This consists of businesses providing information and knowledge-based services, such as:
   - ICT (information and communication technology)
   - consultancy (offering advice to businesses)
   - R&D (research and development).

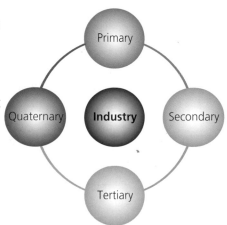
Figure 1.1 The sectors of industry

1

Adding value

Businesses will **add value** to products as they move through the different sectors of industry. For example, a denim jeans manufacturer (secondary sector) will take raw materials such as cotton that they paid £1 for and turn them into a pair of jeans that they sell on for £20. This would represent £19 in added value.

If you think of any product, throughout the stages in bringing that product to market the business at each sector has added value and taken their 'cut' of the profits. This is because they have done something to the product that has made it worth more than when they got it. Another good example is coffee. See Figure 1.2.

Remember

Don't get confused between the different sectors. Learn the difference between 'sectors of industry' and 'sectors of the economy'. A trick to use is to remember that all sectors of industry end in 'ry'!

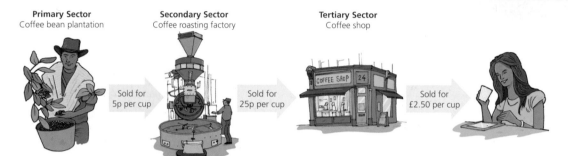

Primary Sector
Coffee bean plantation

Sold for 5p per cup

Secondary Sector
Coffee roasting factory

Sold for 25p per cup

Tertiary Sector
Coffee shop

Sold for £2.50 per cup

Figure 1.2 The three sectors of the coffee industry with £2.45 value added between bean and cup!

Sectors of the economy

There are **three** sectors of the economy:

1 **Private sector**. This consists of businesses that aim primarily to maximise **profits** and includes all profit-making businesses ranging from your local high-street bakery to huge multinational companies such as Ford and Samsung.

2 **Public sector**. This consists of government-owned organisations and agencies which aim to provide a service to society. This sector of the economy includes the NHS, police and state education.

3 **Third sector**. This consists of organisations that have been set up to provide goods or services to benefit others. This sector of the economy includes:
   - charities such as Cancer Research and the SSPCA
   - voluntary organisations such as golf clubs and Scouts groups
   - social enterprises
   - democratic enterprises such as co-operatives.

Private

Economy

Third

Public

Figure 1.3 The sectors of the economy

Remember

... you need to know the main features of all business organisations. This includes ownership, control (who makes decisions), sources of finance, as well as advantages and disadvantages.

Quick questions 1.1 ?

1 Describe the three sectors of the economy.
2 Describe the four sectors of industry.
3 Describe what is meant by adding value and give an example.

What you should know

Features of:
- ★ Public sector organisations
- ★ Private limited companies
- ★ Public limited companies
- ★ Franchises
- ★ Multinationals
- ★ Third sector organisations

The private sector

Private limited companies

Limited companies get their name because they have **limited liability**. This means that owners' personal possessions are not at risk. If the business gets into debt with creditors, the owners only lose their investment in the company. The owners of a limited company are called **shareholders** as they have one or more share in the business. In other words, they share ownership of the business with others. In a **private limited company (Ltd)** shares are not available to the general public and are sold privately to investors whom the business knows, such as employees.

Private limited companies aim to maximise profits, to grow and perhaps increase market share. They are controlled by a **board of directors** who are managed by a managing director. All limited companies have to produce complex documents called the **Memorandum of Association** and **Articles of Association** that outline the rules of the company, such as shareholders' rights and the responsibilities of the directors.

Hints & tips

*Never use complex business jargon like 'limited liability' without describing it. Always define tricky terms like this **in full** to show the examiner you know what you are talking about.*

Table 1.1 Advantages and disadvantages of private limited companies

Advantages	Disadvantages
Owners (shareholders) have limited liability.	Profits have to be split with many shareholders by issuing **dividends**.
Ownership is not lost to outsiders.	A complicated legal process is required to set up the company.
The business usually retains a close and tight-knit, friendly feel with a high level of customer service.	A limited source of capital is available as shares are not sold publicly.
Expertise and business acumen are gained from an experienced board of directors.	Financial statements have to be shared with Companies House (and are therefore made publicly available), meaning profits are not kept private.

Public limited companies

Public limited companies (PLC), like private limited companies, are owned by shareholders who have **limited liability**. They are also controlled by a board of directors. However, unlike private limited companies, public limited companies can sell their shares publicly, through the stock market.

You may have heard of the FTSE 100 (Financial Times Stock Exchange). This is a list of the 100 highest valued PLCs in the UK. Their shares are **traded** (bought and sold) on the London stock exchange. The FTSE 100 contains companies such as Vodafone, Tesco and Sky.

PLCs aim to dominate the market, increase market share and increase market value (the total value of all their shares).

> ## WWW
>
> Take a look at Yahoo's finance pages and find out for yourself about the public limited companies on the London Stock Exchange. You will be amazed at the brands you will recognise:
>
> **https://uk.finance.yahoo.com**

Remember

Remember what the word 'limited' means in limited companies – limited liability!

Table 1.2 Advantages and disadvantages of public limited companies

Advantages	Disadvantages
Shareholders have limited liability.	Dividends are shared with many shareholders.
Large amounts of finance can be raised through the public sale of shares.	Control of the business can be lost as anyone can buy shares on the stock market.
It is easy to borrow finance due to a PLC's size and reputation, so less risk for banks.	Annual accounts have to be published.
PLCs can easily dominate the market.	Setting up a PLC is costly and complicated.

Franchise

A **franchise** is a business model that allows businesses to pay a sum of money to own a branch of a well-known, existing business. The main, original business is known as the **franchiser** and the owner of each individual branch is known as a **franchisee**. Some of the best known franchises are McDonald's, Subway, Papa John's and Red Driving School.

The franchiser's main aim is to grow and increase market share and the franchise model allows this. They also aim to maximise profits and, if they are a PLC, increase their market value too. Each franchisee has very little decision-making power over important strategic and tactical decisions (see Topic 9) as these are made by the main franchiser.

Figure 1.4 Entrepreneurs could choose to run a franchise like Subway rather than start a business from scratch

WWW

Find out for yourself about the franchise opportunities available in the UK. You can read about the financial costs of becoming a franchisee as well as the franchise package and benefits a franchisee would receive at www.franchisedirect.co.uk

Hints & tips

Many students get franchis__er__ and franchis__ee__ mixed up – make sure you are answering about the correct one!

Table 1.3 Advantages and disadvantages of a franchise for the franchiser

Advantages for the *franchiser*	Disadvantages for the *franchiser*
A low-risk form of growth as the franchisee invests the majority of the capital.	The reputation of the whole franchise can be tarnished by one poor franchisee.
Receives a percentage of all franchisee's profits each year (known as **royalties**).	Only a share of profits is received rather than all profits as it would be if they owned each branch.

Table 1.4 Advantages and disadvantages of a franchise for the franchisee

Advantages for the *franchisee*	Disadvantages for the *franchisee*
The franchise is a well-known business with an existing customer base.	There is very little autonomy over decisions as the franchiser decides on products, store layout, uniforms, etc.
Industry knowledge and training is provided by the franchiser.	Royalties have to be paid each year.
The franchisee benefits from national advertisements carried out by the franchiser.	There are high initial start-up fees.

Multinationals

A multinational is a business that has operations in more than one country. This could be worldwide retail outlets such as IKEA or just retail outlets in one country and a production facility in another. Most multinationals are limited companies. Their head office is usually based in the **home country**.

In recent years it has become easier to operate as a multinational due to the improvement in **infrastructure**, for example, inexpensive air travel, single currencies such as the euro, and the growth of e-commerce. All of these have helped the world become one big market place; this is known as **globalisation** and it has helped some multinationals become massively successful.

The effects of multinationals on **host countries** are debatable. On one hand, multinationals provide jobs and training and can have a positive effect on local economies. On the other hand, they can exploit low-paid labour, use up natural resources, put local firms out of business and take their profits back to their home country.

Table 1.5 Advantages and disadvantages of multinationals

Advantages	Disadvantages
Wages and raw material costs are lower in host countries.	Language barriers can slow down communication.
Business can avoid legislation in the home country.	Cultural differences can affect production, e.g. 'siestas' in Spain.
Grants can be issued by governments to locate in their country.	Exchange rates can affect purchasing and paying expenses in different countries.
Business can avoid quotas (retraction on amount of imports/exports) and tariffs (taxes on imports/exports) issued by their own governments.	Time differences can hinder communication between head office and branches around the world.

The public sector

Central government

The UK Government provides national services to the citizens of the UK that it would be very difficult to rely on the private sector to provide. For example, defence by the armed forces, healthcare through the NHS and a transport infrastructure through the road network. These are critical services paid for through **taxation**.

The overall control of policy surrounding these organisations is held by elected politicians. Individual departments are controlled by employed citizens, called civil servants. In Scotland, the Scottish Parliament oversees **devolved** services, such as Education and the Police.

All central government organisations aim to provide a quality service.

The public sector also includes any **nationalised** companies. This means private sector businesses that have been bought in part or in full by the government, to stop them from going bust. An example of this was when the UK Government bought shares in Royal Bank of Scotland (RBS) after the 2008 recession.

The opposite of nationalising is **privatising**, which is selling a public sector organisation to the private sector, for example, when the Royal Mail was floated on the stock market in 2013.

Remember

Many students get confused between the **public sector** and **public limited companies**. They are not the same, in fact, quite the opposite! So why do they both have public in their title? Well, the public sector serves the general *public* for free and public limited companies can sell shares to the general *public*.

Local government

Local government in Scotland is split up into local authorities, such as Fife Council, South Lanarkshire Council, Stirling Council and so on. They provide essential services to the public such as schools, refuse collection and street lighting, free of charge.

Top-level, **strategic** decision-making is carried out by elected councillors, while the **tactical** decisions and **operational** day-to-day running of individual organisations are in the hands of managers and employees of the council, such as the head teacher of your local state secondary school.

Finance comes from taxation collected by central government, local council tax and local business rates. Some organisations, such as council-owned leisure centres, also charge for services to fund running costs.

All local government organisations aim to provide a quality service. They don't aim to make profits; however, some public sector organisations, such as schools, do aim to stick to their given budget and not overspend.

The third sector

Charities

Charities are set up with the sole purpose of raising money to benefit others. They raise finance through donations, sponsorship and fundraising events. They may also have a **trading arm**. This could be through a retail outlet that trades to raise money, such as a high-street Oxfam shop; however, any profits they make are given to their cause rather than kept by the owners. There is no individual owner of a charity; instead it is set up as a **trust**. The overall control of the trust is carried out by a **board of trustees**, while some individual outlets or departments can be managed by paid managers who are assisted by **volunteers**.

The main aims and objectives of charities depend on the individual cause at the heart of the organisation. For instance, the SSPCA (Scottish Society for the Prevention of Cruelty to Animals) aims to improve the welfare of animals in Scotland, while UNICEF aims to protect children's rights worldwide.

Table 1.6 Advantages and disadvantages of charities

Advantages	Disadvantages
Charities are exempt from paying some taxes, such as VAT and Corporation Tax.	It can be difficult to compete with the large marketing budgets of organisations within the private sector.
There are low wage costs due to volunteers working for free.	Charities rely heavily on volunteers who may leave for paid work.
Private companies are more willing to donate to and sponsor charities than ever before as it is good 'PR'.	

Voluntary organisations

Voluntary organisations aim to provide a service for their members and the local community, for example, a local sports club such as a golf club or youth football team. They raise finance mostly through membership subscriptions (sometimes known as 'subs'). They are controlled and run by an **elected committee** and helped by volunteers.

Social enterprises

Social enterprises are organisations that aim to make a profit to benefit a specific group or cause; for example, *The Big Issue* is a magazine that aims to help the homeless in the UK.

Unlike non-profit organisations they operate as private sector businesses do, in that they can be owned by one person (sole trader), two to twenty people (partnership) or shareholders in a limited company. Also, as in the private sector, control can be in the hands of a board of directors or paid managers and finance can come from capital investment or bank loans. However, the main difference between social enterprises and organisations within the private sector is that their profits benefit a social, environmental or cultural cause and not solely the owners of the business.

Table 1.7 Advantages of a social enterprise

Advantages
Social aims can endear a social enterprise to customers.
Good-quality employees who believe in the social 'mission' are attracted to the organisation.
They are likely to receive government grants due to their positive impact on society.
'**Asset lock**' means that, should the enterprise be closed down, the sale of any assets and any profits will be used to benefit their cause.

Case study 1.1
Jamie Oliver's Fifteen

Chef, entrepreneur and TV personality, Jamie Oliver has established a reputable London-based restaurant called Fifteen. The business offers young, unemployed people the experience of learning to work in the restaurant industry. In 2002, Jamie opened the first Fifteen restaurant in London, and recruited 15 young apprentices to train alongside a team of 25 professional chefs. He also set up a charity that would receive all the profits from the restaurant, in order to fund the programme.

Jamie said on the business's website that he was 'particularly excited by the social enterprise model whereby a business is driven primarily by social ambition rather than financial gain'. His vision, which took almost ten years to bring to fruition, was to use the magic of food to give unemployed young people a chance to have a better future.

Figure 1.5 Jamie Oliver is a celebrity chef and entrepreneur

Discussion points

In pairs, groups or on your own, consider:

1 How might society benefit from Jamie Oliver's social enterprise?
2 How can Fifteen and Jamie Oliver's other brands benefit from this social enterprise?

> **WWW**
> Take a look at the social enterprise movement in the UK for yourself at **www.socialenterprise.org.uk**

Democratic enterprises

Increasingly in the EU and USA, democratic enterprises are being developed. All of these businesses share the same objective of generating profit. They differ from private sector businesses in that they aim to make but not necessarily *maximise* profit. Decision-making and profits are shared among members *democratically*. Democratic enterprises are becoming ever more popular with governments which are keen to encourage enterprise and increase wealth in their economy, but which also want their citizens to share in this prosperity.

Co-operatives

A good example of a democratic enterprise is a co-operative, whose main aim is to provide a quality service for the benefit of its members and customers. Co-operatives invite their customers and employees to become members, who then share ownership, decision-making and profits (known as 'dividends').

Co-operatives also subscribe to an internationally agreed set of values and principles, which define their ethical approach to business. These values and principles *and* their democratic structure are what distinguish co-ops from organisations following the social enterprise model.

> **WWW**
> Read more about what a co-operative is at **www.uk.coop/what-co-operative**

Case study 1.2
The Co-operative Group

The best known **co-operative** in the UK is The Co-operative Group (often called the 'Co-op') who have a range of services including food stores, funeral, insurance and legal services. Customers can become members for just £1 and can have a say in decisions, such as how best to help the local community, as well as sharing in any profits.

Figure 1.6 The Co-operative Group is the largest co-operative in the UK

Discussion points

In pairs, groups or on your own, consider:

1   Why might it be good for local communities to have organisations such as The Co-operative Group?
2   In what ways do customers benefit from The Co-operative Group?

Activity 1.1

Wow! I'm sure you will agree that the sectors of the economy topic has a lot of information to take in. This is an important topic that many students find difficult. A good way to summarise the information in this topic is by creating a table like the one below. Try it for yourself.

1   Create a table like the one below, either in your notebook, on your computer or even as an A3 poster.

2   Use the previous pages to gather information about all the features of the main types of business organisations to complete your table.

3   Then try it again, but this time without looking at the book. You may be amazed at how much you remember!

	Private Sector				Public Sector		Third Sector	
	Ltd	PLC	Multinational	Franchise	Central govt.	Local govt.	Charities	Social ent.
Ownership								
Control								
Main finance								
Main aims								
Advantages								
Disadvantages								

Quick questions 1.2

1   Outline three features of a PLC.
2   Describe two third sector organisations.
3   Outline three disadvantages of becoming a multinational.
4   Describe the term 'franchise'.
5   Outline two features of a public sector organisation.

Key question 1.1

Compare two features of a PLC with those of a public sector organisation.

Remember

...to follow the command word (in bold) in the key questions. This is crucial to meet the standard for each outcome.

Objectives

> ## What you should know
>
> ★ Main aims and objectives of each type of organisation
> ★ What organisations do to achieve each objective
> ★ Reasons for changing objectives

Factors affecting objectives

Every organisation will have different aims and objectives depending on a number of factors:

- **Sector of industry**, for example public sector businesses don't want to maximise profits but do want to provide a quality service.
- **Size of organisation**, for example a new start-up company will just want to survive the first year before looking to maximise profits and grow in the future.
- **Changing circumstances**, for example a business might have to respond to the growing need to look environmentally friendly so will have corporate social responsibility as a key objective.

Maximising profits

Making a **profit** means bringing in more money through the business's core activities, such as selling goods and services, than they spend on purchasing materials and other running costs of the business, such as wages and rent. As a business grows it will aim to **maximise profits** which means making as much profit as possible.

Remember

Businesses don't aim to make **money**; they aim to maximize **profits**!

Survival

All private sector businesses and, indeed, third sector businesses aim to **survive**. Survival means avoiding going out of business and having to cease trading. Periods of **economic slowdown** (see Topic 5), such as a recession, are particularly turbulent times for businesses and many fail, even large PLCs.

Satisficing

Satisficing means aiming for a *satisfactory* or adequate result, rather than the best possible outcome. Most private sector businesses would ideally aim to maximise profits; however, through satisficing, a business could aim only to make a level of profit which is good enough to satisfy the main stakeholders, perhaps making enough profit to cover satisfactory dividends to shareholders.

Provide a quality service

All organisations aim to provide a **quality service** to their customers or members. Private sector businesses aim to do this to encourage customers to return and to gain a good reputation and attract new customers. Public sector organisations do this to satisfy the needs of the community and improve the standards of living in their area, such as a school offering a quality education. Third sector organisations want to provide a quality service to aid those individuals or groups they aim to help.

Increasing market share

Market share is the percentage of total sales in a market that a business has. The business that has the most sales in a market is known as the **market leader**. Businesses aim to improve their products and services to ensure that existing customers return *and* to try to entice their rivals' customers to their business. Market share can be illustrated as a pie chart as shown in Figure 1.7.

■ Nike 55%	■ Brooks 5%
■ Asics 11%	■ Saucony 3%
■ Reebok 10%	■ Mizuno 2%
■ Adidas 5%	▢ Puma 2%
■ New Balance 5%	■ Under Armour 1%

Figure 1.7 The US trainers market clearly shows Nike as the market leader

Managerial objectives

Managers within large PLCs or public sector organisations may pursue their own objectives. They may try to achieve objectives which they believe will improve their status within the company, for example, expansion into new markets, or developing new technologies. They may also aim to have many subordinates reporting to them in order to increase their responsibility, and therefore their salary.

Working within a budget

Some organisations will have the objective of sticking to their annual budget and not overspending. This is particularly true for public sector organisations but could be a short-term objective for any organisation when it is struggling in its market and aiming to 'steady the ship' for a while and not make the situation worse.

Sales maximisation

Similar to managerial objectives above, the objective of sales maximisation can arise due to management aiming to achieve personal goals rather than the aims of the business. For example, to **maximise sales** could mean dropping the selling price of a product; managers, salespeople and even entire branches who are on **commission** for the *number* of sales made, will be less interested in the overall profits of the business and more interested in selling as many units as possible.

> ### Hints & tips ⭐
> *Don't ever get 'sales' confused with 'profits'. Sales refers to the number of products sold. Profits refers to how much is made after all costs are deducted.*

Corporate social responsibility

Corporate social responsibility (CSR) refers to organisations aiming to act in an ethical way or in *any* way that benefits either society or the environment.

Methods to ensure good CSR

Ethical and environmental responsibilities (see Topic 20), for example, avoiding the use of child labour.

Philanthropy for example, donating to charity.

Economical responsibilities, for example, using fair and competitive marketing (see Topic 15).

Legal responsibilities, for example, abiding by laws that govern businesses.

Advantages of positive CSR

There are a number of key advantages for a business of having positive CSR:
- The business gains a good reputation for its caring nature.
- Customers who agree with the aim are likely to use the business.
- The business can attract high-quality staff who believe in the ethics of the business.
- Society and the environment are kept in good order, which will benefit the business in the long run.

Case study 1.3

Lush

Lush is a huge multinational company that specialises in fresh handmade cosmetics. Despite its size, it is an organisation with positive CSR at its heart. Just take a look at this screenshot from its website.

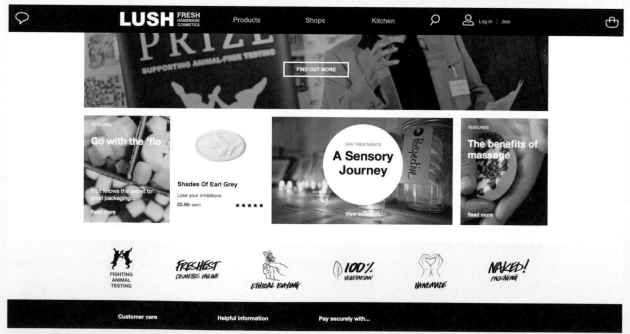

Figure 1.8 Lush website showing its commitment to CSR

Lush is now renowned for its active campaigns against animal testing. It uses fair trade products, encourages recycling and low-waste packaging, and it donates to charity through selling 'Charity Pot', a hand and body lotion.

It has even set up its own charitable fund, called the 'SLush Fund'. Two per cent of the total amount Lush spends on raw materials and packaging is donated to the fund. This money is then used to start sustainable farming and community projects from scratch, some of which produce and process ingredients for its products.

$\Rightarrow$

Discussion points

In pairs, groups or on your own, consider:

1   How many examples of good CSR can you spot in the single screenshot?
2   Why should more organisations aim to be as thorough about CSR as Lush?

Quick questions 1.3

1   Describe the term 'CSR'.
2   Suggest three methods to improve CSR.
3   Using examples, give two reasons why all organisations have different objectives.

Growth

After starting up, a successful business will aim to grow. To 'grow' means to make the business larger. Not all organisations will aim to grow. Local government organisations, for example, aim instead to serve the local community; growing is not of interest to them. Some private limited companies like to stay small too, as their customers like the personal touch that bigger franchises and multinationals cannot offer. However, if a business does grow it will realise a number of advantages.

Table 1.8 The advantages of growth

Advantage	Explanation
Reduces the risk of failure	Bigger businesses with more products or branches can spread the risk and avoid 'putting all their eggs in one basket'.
Increases profits	More products to sell or more stores to sell them in will equal more sales, and more profits.
Avoids being taken over	Bigger businesses aim to buy smaller businesses to control their products, outlets and customers. By growing larger, a business can be the 'big fish in the pond' and avoid being eaten itself.
Removes competition	Bigger businesses can put smaller ones out of business and this can significantly increase the market share of the bigger business.
Economies of scale	Bigger businesses can benefit purely from being so large, for example: ● **Bulk buying**. The more materials a business purchases, the cheaper the unit cost is. Just as when you buy a multipack of crisps, the unit cost (cost per individual bag) is cheaper than when you buy a single bag. ● **Finance**. Finance is easier to obtain from banks and interest is at a lower rate than for smaller businesses. ● **Specialist functions**. Large businesses can afford to have specialist departments (known as 'functions'). For instance having a dedicated marketing department with expert staff will mean promotions will be more effective than those of smaller businesses.

Topic 4
Methods of growth

Methods of growth

Internal/Organic growth

This means businesses deciding to grow on their own without getting involved with other organisations. Growing in this way will increase market share without losing control of the business to outsiders. See Table 1.9 for more information about internal/organic growth methods.

Table 1.9 Internal/organic growth methods

Internal/Organic growth method	Description
Launching new products/services	Businesses can meet the needs of different market segments, especially if they **diversify**, i.e. launch new products into different markets from their current ones or export existing products abroad.
Opening new branches or expanding existing branches	A business can reach new markets by opening up in new locations. It can also expand existing premises to cater for more products/staff and more customers, make more sales.
Introducing e-commerce	By selling online, a business can trade 24/7 to a global market.
Hiring more staff	Increasing the number of staff will improve the business's ability to make sales, make better decisions and develop more products.
Increasing production capacity	Businesses can invest in new technology to make more products themselves.

Diversification

This is when products are launched across different markets, for example Samsung sell mobile phones, tablets and TVs but also refrigerators and washing machines. Clearly this increases potential customers and spreads risk across different markets; however, it does require numerous resources to offer such a vast product range, i.e. the business may need to use a **product grouping**.

Horizontal integration

Horizontal integration occurs when two businesses from the *same* sector of industry become one business. This could be two dairy farms **merging** (primary sector) or one bank **taking over** another bank (tertiary sector).

Table 1.10 Advantages and disadvantages of horizontal integration

Advantages	Disadvantages
The new, larger business can dominate the market as competition will be vastly reduced.	The merger/takeover may breach EU competition rules.
The new business can benefit from economies of scale, e.g. buying in bulk to reduce prices.	Quality may suffer due to lack of competition.
Due to reduced competition, the new larger business can raise prices, increasing profits.	Customers may have to pay higher prices for the same goods.

Forward vertical integration

Vertical integration occurs when two businesses from *different* sectors of industry become one business. When vertically integrated businesses separate it is known as **deintegration**.

Forward vertical integration is when a business takes over or merges with a business in a *later* sector of industry, often a distributor. An example would be a manufacturer of mobile phones, such as HTC, taking over a mobile phone shop, such as Carphone Warehouse.

Normally a secondary business (for example, a mobile phone manufacturer) would sell goods to a tertiary business (for example, a mobile phone shop) at trade price, allowing the tertiary business to add on a margin of profit to the retail price they sell the product at. After taking over a tertiary business, the secondary business is able to sell their product directly to customers for the more expensive retail price, therefore **adding value** to their selling price and increasing profits.

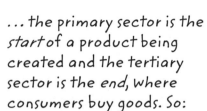

Remember

... the primary sector is the start of a product being created and the tertiary sector is the end, where consumers buy goods. So:

☞ *forward* vertical integration: moving closer to the consumer.
☞ *backward* vertical integration: moving back towards the raw materials.

Backward vertical integration

Backward vertical integration is when a business takes over or merges with a business in an *earlier* sector of industry, in other words they take over their supplier. An example would be a coffee company, such as Starbucks, taking over a coffee bean plantation.

Table 1.11 The different advantages and shared disadvantages of forward vertical and backward vertical integration

Advantages of forward vertical integration	● The business can control supply of its products and could decide to not supply to competition. ● Can increase profits by 'cutting out the middle man' and **adding value** itself.
Advantages of backward vertical integration	● Guaranteed and timely supply of inventory (stock). ● No need to pay a supplier its marked-up prices so inventory is cheaper. ● Quality of supplies can be strictly controlled.
Disadvantages of both backward vertical and forward vertical integration	● Company may be incapable of managing new activities efficiently, meaning higher costs. ● Focusing on new activities can adversely affect core activities. ● Monopolising markets may have legal repercussions.

Lateral integration

This is when a business acquires or merges with a business that is in the same industry but does not provide the exact same product. In other words, the two businesses are not in direct competition with each other. An example would be if Greggs bought a wedding cake bakery. They are both 'bakeries' but very different types of bakery and are not competing for the same custom. Another example is when Google bought YouTube. See Figure 1.10 to see lateral integration illustrated along with the other types of integration.

Google

Google Search   I'm Feeling Lucky

Figure 1.9 Google bought YouTube, which was an example of lateral integration

Table 1.12 Advantages and disadvantages of lateral integration

Advantages	Disadvantages
The business can target new markets and therefore increase sales.	The lack of knowledge in a slightly different market may affect the performance of the products.
New products can complement existing ones, e.g. if a suit company bought a shirt maker both could then be sold as a complete outfit for a customer to wear.	It may adversely affect core activities.

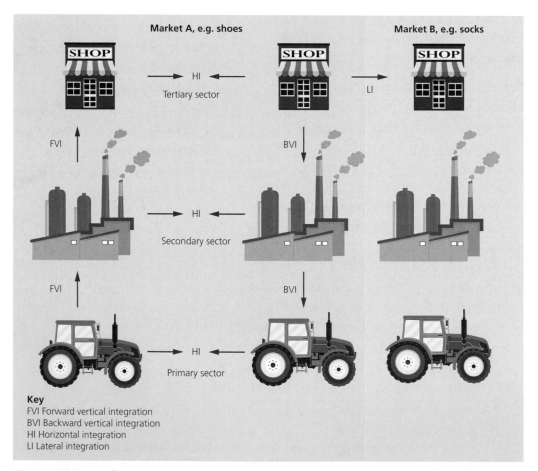

Figure 1.10 Types of integration

Conglomerate integration

Conglomerate integration occurs when businesses in different markets join together; in other words, a merger of businesses whose activities are totally unrelated. Businesses do this primarily to spread the risk of failure, but they will also, of course, increase their chances of maximising profits by having more and varied products and services for sale.

Table 1.13 Advantages and disadvantages of conglomerate integration

Advantages	Disadvantages
The business can spread risk. If one market fails, the losses can be compensated for by profits in another.	One business may take on another in a market they know nothing about and this may cause the new business to fail.
It can overcome seasonal fluctuations in their markets and have more consistent year-round sales.	Having too many products across different markets can cause the company to lose focus on core activities, impacting on other products.
The business is larger and therefore more financially secure.	The business may become too large and inefficient to manage.
The buyer acquires the assets of the other company.	
The business gains the customers and sales of the acquired business.	

Case study 1.4
Procter & Gamble

Procter & Gamble (P&G) is the world's largest consumer goods conglomerate. You may never have heard of P&G but you will have heard of many of their brands! They include Ariel, Duracell, Pantene Pro V, Oral B, Olay, Gillette and many, many more! P&G, like most conglomerates, managed to get so huge by taking over or merging with lots of other businesses over a number of years. Gillette is one of their most recent acquisitions and is a perfect example of conglomerate integration.

Figure 1.11 A range of P&G's products

Before the merger, P&G's product portfolio largely omitted the male grooming market and Gillette was the market leader. By taking over Gillette, P&G overcame a tough barrier to entering the market (that is Gillette's large market share), gained its brand name and, of course, all of its customers!

Discussion points

In pairs, groups or on your own, consider:

1 What might the benefits be to P&G of having so many brands in so many markets?
2 Why do you think P&G bought Gillette?

Activity 1.2

1 On your own or in pairs, identify or find out using the internet which type of integration the following recent examples are:
   a) Amazon taking over Lovefilm and renaming it Prime Video
   b) Coca-Cola buying innocent smoothies
   c) Apple buying up various processor-chip manufacturers
   d) Universal buying a chain of cinemas
   e) Tui merging with First Choice
   f) Volkswagen taking over Porsche
   g) Virgin taking over publishing company Random House
   h) L'Oréal buying The Body Shop
   i) Google buying a wind farm.

WWW

Take a look at the Procter & Gamble website and see their large and varied product portfolio for yourself: **www.pg.com**

2 a) Using the internet or the business sections of a quality newspaper, find out some examples of integration of your own.
   b) Ask your teacher or lecturer to check if you have correctly identified the types of integration.
   c) Present your findings as a poster, showing clearly the old logos becoming the new logos and annotating with information about the type of integration, advantages, disadvantages, and so on.

Ways to achieve growth

Takeovers and mergers

A **takeover** involves one business (usually a larger business) buying another (usually smaller) business. This can often be hostile and comes as a result of the smaller business struggling financially and the larger business exploiting the situation. Takeovers (also known as **acquisitions**) sometimes result in the smaller business's stores or outlets taking the name of the larger one, as was the case when Spanish bank Santander took over Abbey National. Sometimes the larger company just wants to add another product or service to its portfolio, for example, when Google bought YouTube.

Table 1.14 Advantages and disadvantages of takeovers

Advantages	Disadvantages
The buying business gains the market share and resources of the taken-over business.	Integration can lead to job losses in the taken-over business as the buying business wants its own management and employees.
Risk of failure can be spread.	If the buying business moves the headquarters or production to its home country/area, this can have a bad effect on the taken-over business's local economy.
Economies of scale can be achieved.	Integration can be bad for customers as less competition means higher prices.
Competition is reduced, which will increase sales.	A change of name can put off loyal customers of the taken-over business.
	It can be expensive to acquire another business.

Case study 1.5

Coca-Cola–Costa

In 2018 Coca-Cola agreed to take over Costa Coffee for £3.9 billion from Whitbread, which had bought the chain for 'just' £19 million. Why did Coca-Cola agree to pay so much? Firstly, the coffee industry is booming. While other high-street industries struggle to compete with the internet, people still like 'going for a coffee' and that trend is set to continue. Secondly, while Coca-Cola is a giant of soft drinks, owning brands such as Fanta, Powerade and innocent, it doesn't have a hot drink brand in its portfolio. Thirdly, the soft drinks industry is shrinking as customers move away from drinks seen as unhealthy. Fourthly, Coca-Cola doesn't currently have any physical outlets so it could sell its existing drinks in the 4000 Costa shops throughout the world!

Discussion points

In pairs, groups or on your own:
1 Analyse the costs and benefits to Coca-Cola of taking over Costa.
2 Suggest reasons why the coffee industry is set to keep growing.
3 Suggest ways that the takeover could help Costa close the gap on the market leader, Starbucks.

Case study 1.6

Disney–Pixar

Up until the launch of *Cars*, Disney had used Pixar, experts in computer animation and owned by the late Steve Jobs, to produce its CGI (computer generated imagery) movies using **outsourcing** (see page 22). Then Disney, rather than paying Pixar for collaborations, wanted the two businesses to become one. Disney paid more than £4 billion to acquire Pixar; it was not a hostile takeover but more like a merger in that it benefited both sides. Disney secured the exclusive services of the best CGI company and Steve Jobs became a majority shareholder and got a seat on the Disney board. This is just one of Disney's many acquisitions that has made it a massive company. Disney has taken over Marvel, Star Wars and even a major league baseball team!

Figure 1.12 Disney now own Marvel

Discussion points

In pairs, groups or on your own, consider:

1   Why do you think Disney and Pixar merged?
2   How could Disney have benefited from NOT buying Pixar?
3   What will be the benefits to Disney of their takeover of Marvel and the Star Wars empire?

A **merger** involves two businesses agreeing to join forces and become one organisation. This is often friendlier than a takeover and can result in a new name and logo for the new, merged organisation.

Table 1.15 Advantages and disadvantages of mergers

Advantages	Disadvantages
Market share and resources are shared, which can spread risk of failure and increase profits.	Customers may dislike the changes a merger may bring e.g. new logo, new name etc … as the familiarity of the previous businesses are lost.
Economies of scale can be achieved.	Marketing campaigns to inform customers of changes can be expensive.
Each business can bring different areas of expertise to the merger.	Can be bad for customers as less competition will mean higher prices.
Unlike a takeover, jobs are more likely to be spared in both businesses.	
Can overcome barriers to entering a market, such as strong competition.	

Other ways to achieve growth

- Franchising
- Becoming a multinational
- Internal growth, e.g. new staff, new products

Ways of funding growth

Retained profits

The first way of funding growth is through the use of **retained profits**. These are any profits made by the business that aren't given to shareholders. They are kept in the business to fund growth, such as developing new products.

Remember

*… that there is a difference between the **methods** of growth, the **ways to achieve** growth and the **ways of funding** growth. Make sure you know what comes under each heading.*

Divestment

Divestment is selling off part of an organisation, such as a subsidiary company or one of the company's brands. An organisation may divest because it wishes to concentrate on other, more profitable areas of the business, focus on a specific target market or simply cash in on selling part of the organisation. A previously de-merged component that is then sold off is an example of divestment.

Remember

… divestment is the opposite of investment. In other words, selling part of the business rather than buying a new part of the business.

Case study 1.7

Pringles

Remember Procter & Gamble, the large conglomerate responsible for many famous household brands? Well, as you would expect for such a large company, as well as taking over and merging with many businesses throughout the years, they have also **divested** too. P&G had only one food brand in its portfolio, Pringles crisps. In 2012, they divested the brand and sold it to Kellogg's. So why would they divest such a profitable and famous brand?

● They received a *huge* sum of money, £2.75 billion to be exact!
● They decided to concentrate on their 'core activities', such as domestic cleaning, beauty and grooming.
● They could invest the profits from the sale of Pringles into their other markets.

Discussion points

In pairs, groups or on your own:

1   Can you think of any reasons why P&G should have held on to Pringles?
2   Explain, in the context of P&G divesting Pringles, what is meant by 'concentrating on core activities'.

Deintegration

This is when a business sells off part of the supply chain that it owns. It occurs when a business has become vertically integrated with either its supplier or customer and eventually realises that it would be better off as separate businesses. An example of deintegration would be if Tesco sold Booker, a wholesale business (one of Tesco's suppliers) that it recently took over.

Table 1.16 Advantages and disadvantages of deintegration

Advantages	Disadvantages
The business can focus on core activities, for example if it is a manufacturer it can focus on making rather than farming or selling.	The business will now have to pay marked-up prices for supplies.
There is increased choice in the 'vertical chain' as the business can now look for supplies or customers outside its organisation.	Competitors could acquire deintegrated components and take control of the supply chain.

Asset stripping

This is taking over another company with intent to sell off its assets for a profit. The individual assets of the organisation, such as factories, retail spaces or fleet, may be more valuable than the organisation as a whole.

Asset stripping can cause the buyers to gain a bad reputation as this often happens after a hostile takeover, with the profitable remains of the business being sold off, bit by bit, and the non-profitable areas being closed down.

De-merger

A **de-merger** occurs when a single business splits into two or more separate components. The de-merged components are still owned by the same organisation as before; however, they are managed independently of each other.

Table 1.17 Advantages and disadvantages of de-mergers

Advantages	Disadvantages
Each new 'component' can concentrate on its own core activities and grow as a result.	Customers may be put off by the de-merger and abandon the businesses altogether.
Each new component has the best chance to operate efficiently.	There are significant financial costs involved, for example, in re-branding shop fronts, marketing campaigns to inform customers of the change, and so on.
De-merged components can be **divested** which can meet competition regulations, set by the EU.	

Case study 1.8
Lloyds TSB

In 2013 Lloyds TSB – an organisation that existed due to a previous merger in 1995 of Lloyds Bank and TSB – announced that it was splitting into two separate banks: Lloyds Bank and TSB. This came after the EU, under new competition rules, judged in 2009 that greater competition was to be created within the UK banking industry. The advantages of this for customers include better services and more attractive interest rates.

After the initial **de-merger** in 2013, in 2014 Lloyds Banking Group **divested** TSB when it was sold on the stock market. Lloyds Bank and TSB now have an opportunity to focus on more specific products that will respond to the needs of the customers in the target markets they identify. An example of this is TSB's stated commitment to 'local banking' whereby each new branch will focus on 'local customers, local businesses and local communities' and money belonging to local communities stays in local communities in the UK.

Discussion points

In pairs, groups or on your own, consider:

1 Why do you think the EU judged that Lloyds Banking Group had to de-merge?
2 Using the context of the case study distinguish between the terms de-merger and divestment.
3 Suggest advantages for customers of more choice in the market.

Management buy-out/buy-in

A **buy-out** is when the management of a business buy the company they work for. A **buy-in** is when the management of another business, usually a competitor, takes over the business. In both cases, the management team will feel they have the ideas and industry knowledge to turn the business around and make it successful.

Outsourcing

Outsourcing, also known as **contracting-out**, is when an organisation arranges for another organisation to carry out certain activities for it, instead of doing it itself. A business could outsource its administration, IT work, printing, legal services, marketing or accountancy. Your school may outsource its catering to a specialist catering company. An organisation will generally do this to concentrate on **core activities**.

> **Remember**
>
> Concentrating on core activities is a useful phrase to remember; it is a benefit of many ways to fund growth looked at here.

Table 1.18 Advantages and disadvantages of outsourcing

Advantages	Disadvantages
Outsourcing allows the business to concentrate on doing what it is good at, rather than getting bogged down with additional services.	The business will have less control over outsourced work so quality may fall.
Less labour and equipment is required for outsourced activities, for example, outsourcing printing saves on printers and reprographics staff.	Communication between the businesses needs to be very clear to make sure exact specifications are met.
There should be high-quality work from the outsourced business as it should have greater expertise and specialist equipment.	The business may have to share sensitive information with the outsourced business that could get into the hands of competitors.
The outsourced business may provide the service cheaper than an in-house department could as it can benefit from economies of scale, doing the same work for many other businesses.	Outsourcing could be more expensive than in-house as specialists and expertise come at a price.
The business is able to use the service when it is required, so saving costs on idle staff and machinery.	

Quick questions 1.4 ?

1. Describe two advantages of growth for a business.
2. Other than using retained profits, suggest three ways of funding growth.
3. Describe the term 'deintegration'.
4. Outline two disadvantages of backward vertical integration.
5. Describe the difference between a buy-out and a buy-in.

Key questions 1.2 ?

1. **Identify** two objectives a PLC would have.
2. **Justify** the importance of the objectives you identified above.

External factors

Factors and their impact

External factors are the different situations that impact on the success of
an organisation that arise *outside* the organisation. The organisation can't
control external factors.

Political factors

Political factors affecting organisations arise from
decisions made and actions taken by the
government, either at a local or national level. This
can be changes in laws and legislation, or
alterations to a government's **fiscal policy** which
impacts upon spending in an economy by altering
tax rates and levels of public spending. The
following table highlights both the positive and
negative impacts of a selection of political factors
on an organisation.

Remember

*... the external
factors with the
mnemonic PESTEC.*

Figure 1.13 Government spending on Edinburgh trams
improved infrastructure for local businesses

Table 1.19 Impact of political factors

Political factor	Positive impact	Negative impact
Changing laws and legislation	The government could introduce environmental protection laws and policies such as 'Zero Waste Scotland' and, by complying, organisations will be seen in good light. This is good PR and can attract potential customers.	The government could increase the minimum wage so that organisations have higher wage costs. This will result in a lower profit for the year.
Changing income tax rates	The government could reduce taxes (money collected by the government to fund public spending), such as income tax. This will give customers a higher disposable income. This means customers will be more likely to buy products.	The government could increase income tax. This will give customers a lower disposable income. This means customers would be less likely to spend money on a business's products, unless it is essential. This will reduce sales overall.
Changing VAT rates	The government could lower VAT (value added tax). This is a tax on goods and services. Reducing the VAT rate will make products more affordable for customers, increasing sales for a business.	The government could raise VAT. This will increase the selling price which could put customers off purchasing products and reduce sales.

Political factor	Positive impact	Negative impact
Changing corporation tax	Many types of businesses, such as limited companies, have to pay a tax on their profits (corporation tax). The government could lower the rate of corporation tax which would mean less money is taken from the business and given to the government, which would increase profits.	The government could raise the rate of corporation tax which means more money would be taken from the business and given to the government, which would reduce the profit of the organisation.
Public spending on infrastructure	The government could decide to fund the development of infrastructure. Examples include building new motorways, car parks, tram networks, and so on. This will increase the likelihood of attracting customers for businesses in these areas. Public spending also creates jobs, which gives people wages and enables them to spend money on other goods and services.	Public spending is a contentious issue as it only improves certain areas. For example, the Edinburgh tram network greatly improved Edinburgh's infrastructure; however, businesses in Glasgow saw no benefit. This is known as 'opportunity cost', i.e. the cost of spending money on one area is that it can't be spent in another.

Competition policy

In 2014, the **Competition and Markets Authority** (CMA) was launched by the UK government. Its aim is to investigate markets and enforce **competition policy** in order to promote competition for the benefit of consumers.

Reasons for promoting competition

It is in the government's interest to promote competition for the following reasons:
- prices are kept low for consumers
- products and services are high quality
- customer service is good
- entire markets improve and grow, creating jobs and raising GDP see page 25
- healthy markets can attract foreign investment.

Impact of competition policy

Here are just some of the areas that competition policy covers and the impact it has on businesses:
- **Cartels** – Organisations cannot participate in **cartels**. This means colluding with other organisations to fix prices to make higher profits. If found guilty of participating in cartels, owners or management can be fined or even sentenced to prison.
- **Mergers** – The CMA can block mergers if it is likely to lead to a 'substantial lessening of competition' in any market. The CMA can also impose conditions that must be met for a merger to be given the green light. For example, when the CMA investigated the Sainsbury's/Asda merger they forced them to divest (sell) a number of stores, mostly to Morrisons, to ensure there was enough competition in certain towns.

- **Anti-competitive behaviour** – Organisations cannot use their dominant position in the market to charge drastically low prices, pay lower prices to suppliers or control the supply of goods to the detriment of the market.
- **Consumer protection** – Consumers have rights and are protected from unfair practices such as hidden charges and poor customer service.

WWW

Read more about competition policy and the CMA: **www. gov.uk/government/ organisations/ competition-and- markets-authority**

Economic factors

Economic cycle

Economic factors arise from the state of the **economy**. An economy is the state of a country or region in terms of the production and consumption of products, and the supply of money. In other words, when the UK economy is doing well, businesses produce more products, which creates more jobs and leads to more people having more money to spend. However, the economy alternates between good and bad times. You will perhaps remember the global **recession** that hit in 2008, when unemployment was high and businesses were going bust. This economic activity is known as the **economic cycle** and is illustrated in Figure 1.14.

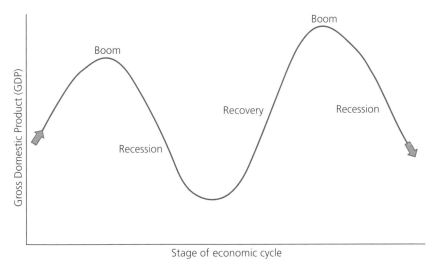

Figure 1.14 The economic cycle

Remember

This can be quite tricky, but the bottom line is that **booms** are good for businesses and **recessions** are bad!

The economic cycle diagram illustrates the different stages of an economy in terms of a country's **gross domestic product (GDP)**. GDP is a figure that sums up the amount of goods and services produced and consumed by a country, so GDP is a good indicator not only of output and profits of businesses, but also of employment and the wealth of citizens too. Table 1.20 describes each stage of the economic cycle and the impact of each stage on businesses.

Table 1.20 Impact of the economic cycle stages

Stage	Definition	Impact
Boom	GDP and employment levels are very high.	Businesses can take advantage of the demand for products and the wealth of consumers by increasing prices. This will improve profits for the business.
	Demand for products is high.	However, a side effect is an increase in **inflation**. This is a rise in prices over time and often leads to wage rises, so people can afford to keep up with inflation.
Recession	GDP and employment levels fall.	Businesses have to react to a falling demand by making staff redundant, which will cost them redundancy payments and lose them the skills and knowledge of employees.
	Demand for products falls.	Prices will have to be cut to try and increase demand, which will lower the amount of profit a business can make and may even lead to losses.
Recovery	GDP and employment levels begin to rise.	Businesses can rely on consumers being in a better position to spend money due to rising employment, so therefore sales will increase.
	Demand for products increases.	Businesses can develop new products and start to increase prices, which will lead to bigger profits for the business.

Economic policy

It is the role of the government to try and control the economy through a number of measures, called economic policy. The **economic policy** of a government can be divided into two areas, fiscal policy and monetary policy.

1 **Fiscal policy** – A government's fiscal policy concerns the tax rates it sets and its level of public spending (as covered in the political section of external factors).

2 **Monetary policy** – A government's monetary policy is the ways in which it controls the supply of money into the economy and therefore affects spending. This can be done by varying **interest rates**.

Interest rates

Interest rates determine the percentage that is added to borrowings or savings. All financial institutions, such as banks or building societies, set their own interest rates. However, the government bank, the Bank of England, sets the **base rate** of interest. This is the minimum rate of interest that banks and building societies *must* apply to loans and savings.

By increasing interest rates the Bank of England attempts to curb spending and therefore reduce inflation.

By decreasing interest rates the Bank of England attempts to encourage spending in order to avoid a recession or to recover the economy. Table 1.21 highlights how this is achieved and the impact of interest rate changes on businesses.

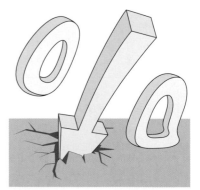

Figure 1.15 A drop in interest rates encourages consumer spending

Table 1.21 The impact on business of changes in interest rates

Interest rate	Effect on savings	Effect on borrowing
Rise in interest rate	Customers are *more* likely to save due to attractive rates as they will earn more money on their savings. This means customers will spend less on businesses' products as they are saving their money instead.	Customers are *less* likely, or able, to take out loans or to spend using credit cards as they will have to pay back more money on their borrowing. This means customers will be able to spend less on businesses' products.
Reduction in interest rate	Customers are *less* likely to save as interest rates are unattractive, so are more likely to spend money on businesses' products.	Customers are *more* likely to borrow money as it is less expensive to pay back loans and credit card debts, so are more likely to spend money on businesses' products.

Exchange rates

An **exchange rate** determines the amount of one currency that can be bought using another currency. For example, if the exchange rate of £ (pounds sterling) to the € (euro) is 1.25, it means for every £1 exchanged, €1.25 is given. The exchange rate of the pound sterling against foreign currencies changes on a daily basis.

A high value or 'strong' pound is caused by a high demand for the currency. If UK products are selling well abroad (known as **exports**) the pound will be in demand and the price will rise. The Bank of England can affect this too through interest rates, as high interest rates will attract savings from abroad and again the price of the pound will rise. Of course, the opposite is also true – a high demand for goods purchased from abroad (**imports**), low demand for exports and low interest rates will cause the demand for the pound to fall and therefore the price of the pound to fall too. Table 1.22 highlights the effect of exchange rate changes on businesses.

Table 1.22 The effects of exchange rate changes on businesses

Exchange rate	Effect on exports	Effect on imports
Strong pound	If the value of the pound is high compared to foreign currencies, UK exporters will struggle to sell their products abroad as they will be more expensive than foreign goods and sales will fall.	If the value of the pound is high compared to foreign currencies, imports will become cheaper. This will decrease costs for businesses that source materials from abroad which will increase their profits. It will also allow a lower selling price to be charged for products made in the UK to attract customers.
Weak pound	If the value of the pound is low compared to foreign currencies, UK exporters will be able to sell more goods to foreign countries as their goods will be less expensive for customers outside the UK.	If the value of the pound is low compared to foreign currencies, imports will become more expensive. This will increase costs for businesses that source their materials from abroad and may lead to an increase in prices.

European Union

Britain leaving the European Union, known as **Brexit**, has various impacts on UK businesses:

- Businesses **exporting** to the EU will have lower profits due to **tariffs** (these are taxes placed on goods crossing borders) that don't have to be paid when goods are exchanged in the EU.

- Prices of materials bought from EU countries will be dearer, again due to increased **tariffs** as a result of not being part of the EU.
- There will no longer be free movement of labour so businesses will struggle to attract the best talent from abroad.

On the other hand:

- Without the restriction of the EU, UK businesses could be able to trade without **tariffs** and **quotas** (restrictions on the amount of goods that can cross borders). This means they could trade more freely with other markets, such as China and the world's largest economy, the USA.
- The pound will be weaker, which means industries such as tourism will benefit, see Table 1.22 above.

Social factors

Social factors concern the ways in which *society* changes and the need for businesses to adapt in the same way. Social factors could be either a change in the **demographics**, the characteristics of the population, or a change in cultural behaviour. Table 1.23 highlights a selection of social factors and their possible impact on organisations.

www

The UK, and indeed the world, economy is always changing. It would be beneficial for your Higher Business Management studies for you to keep up to date with changes that are taking place and how these changes impact on organisations. You can keep informed at the following website: **www.economist.com**

Table 1.23 The effects of social factors on businesses

Social factor	Positive impact	Negative impact
UK's ageing population	This is a vast, and growing, market segment. Businesses that can produce products tailored for this market should succeed. Many potential customers in this segment are retired and well off so there is a potential to offer quality products at high prices.	Extensive market research must be carried out which costs time and money.
More women with professional careers	As more women are taking up high-profile professions and managerial roles they are waiting longer to have a family. As a result, couples are generally better off when they have their first child so businesses can offer high-quality maternity and baby products that sell for a high price.	More women will be taking maternity leave once they are established in their careers which will mean organisations have to consider flexible working arrangements, such as part time or job share. This will result in the organisation having to spend time recruiting and training replacement staff.
Evolving work–life balance	Fewer employees are working the traditional 9–5 working week. As a result, businesses must cater for the needs of a society that works around the clock for 7 days a week. This has led to a trend of convenience in the UK, e.g. 24-hour opening hours, e-commerce, etc. By meeting the convenience needs of customers businesses will ensure repeat custom.	Organisations have to provide more staff to work 24 hours a day, 7 days a week to meet customer needs, which will increase wage costs.
Changing fashion trends	Businesses can cater for the latest fashion trends and offer products that customers want, therefore increasing sales. For example the North Face or Supreme clothing trend.	Businesses have to spend time and money researching and developing new products. Some products also have a very short shelf-life.

Social factor	Positive impact	Negative impact
Flexible working arrangements	Flexible working arrangements mean staff will be able to work at a time when they are most productive, which will improve quality in the organisation as well as raising morale. Additionally, businesses can save money on renting office space if more employees work from home.	Flexible working arrangements can lead to a lack of supervision and direction of staff, which can reduce productivity. Organisations may also have to provide staff with equipment such as smartphones and laptops so they can work at home, which can be costly.
Ethical considerations	Businesses that practice **ethically** (doing what is right) will be seen in a good light by customers, prospective employees, suppliers and the government. An example would be not exploiting child labour.	Often unethical practice is carried out purely to keep costs low so operating ethically will increase costs and perhaps reduce overall profits. Of course, a bad image from operating unethically could affect sales anyway!

Technological factors

Technological factors concern the quickly evolving technological advancements that can impact on organisations, for example, faster broadband connections, cloud computing and social media. Table 1.24 highlights a selection of technological factors and the possible impact on organisations.

Figure 1.16 Cloud computing is changing the way people work

Remember

Technology can be an internal or an external factor. The main difference is that as an internal factor the concern is existing technology, which is the technology the business uses already, while as an external factor the concern is keeping up with technological developments, that is what technology the business needs to invest in to remain competitive. More specific uses of technology are covered throughout this book.

Table 1.24 The effects of technological factors on businesses

Technological factor	Positive impact	Negative impact
Cloud computing	Through technology such as OneDrive or Dropbox, organisations can save money on their own IT hardware. Additionally, they will not require as many IT staff to maintain equipment, saving on wage costs.	There is a heavy reliance on 'the cloud' performing. If internet connection is unavailable, the organisation won't be able to access files stored on the cloud, causing production to stop. There are also privacy and confidentiality issues regarding storing information on the cloud.
Social media	Having a social media (e.g. Facebook, Twitter) presence enables organisations to keep in touch with customers and raise their profile to a potentially worldwide market.	Social media can be used by customers to spread bad reviews about an organisation, leading to a poor reputation that could put customers off and cause them to take their business to the competition.
Wi-Fi	Organisations that provide a free Wi-Fi service are likely to attract customers who wish to use Wi-Fi for work or personal reasons, for example a customer choosing a Starbucks coffee house over an independent coffee shop because of Starbucks' free Wi-Fi.	There is a financial cost of setting up and maintaining Wi-Fi.
4G	4G will enable organisations' employees to communicate and download information while on the move much more quickly.	Not all areas are equipped with 4G capabilities, which could leave organisations in these areas behind.

Environmental factors

Environmental factors can either arise from the ways in which the natural environment impacts on organisations or the ways that organisations act in an ethical and environmentally friendly manner. Table 1.25 highlights a selection of environmental factors and the possible impact on organisations.

Table 1.25 The effects of environmental factors on businesses

Environmental factor	Positive impact	Negative impact
Weather	A business could be impacted by spells of favourable weather, for example, during prolonged periods of snow the ski industry in Scotland will see an increase in customers.	Prolonged spells of adverse weather, such as snow, can affect the transport networks across the UK. This will make it difficult for deliveries of materials to arrive and for staff to get to work, therefore causing production to slow down or cease entirely.
Recycling	Organisations encourage recycling by their customers in order to impact less negatively on the environment. For example, retailers discourage the use of plastic bags and sell 'bags for life' which will lower the cost to the retailer of providing plastic bags and gain the company a favourable reputation for being 'environmentally friendly'.	Organisations need to undertake recycling, for example, of waste paper and printer cartridges, but it takes time, effort and money to recycle rather than just disposing of waste.
Carbon footprint	Organisations are encouraged to reduce their carbon footprint. This means to lower the amount of emissions from fossil fuels released into the atmosphere. Businesses that do this, for example by utilising renewable energy, will eventually save money on fuel bills.	There is a financial cost associated with investing in renewable energy, for example, solar panels or wind turbines to power factories.

Competitive factors

Most businesses face **competition**. An organisation's competition refers to rival organisations that provide the same or a similar product and attempt to take their customers, attract new customers or keep their own customers. Many methods used by competition will be covered in the **marketing** chapter (see Chapter 2) but a select few examples are given in Table 1.26, including some positive ways that competition can impact on an organisation.

Table 1.26 The effects of competitive factors on businesses

Positive impacts	Negative impacts
Competition opening up a physical store right next to a business can be good as it provides more choice for customers and brings passing trade to the area.	The competition could lower prices, undercutting another business. Businesses will either have to lower prices too, reducing profits, or risk losing customers to the competition.
Competition improves a market as it brings with it more choice, new ideas and keeps prices low, which can benefit all businesses in the market.	The competition could launch new or improved products. Businesses will have to spend money researching and developing products to keep up with competition.

Activity 1.3

External factors, or PESTEC analysis, is a great way to *analyse* the threats and opportunities to an organisation that exist in the external environment.

1   Create a presentation using PowerPoint, Prezi, a mind-map, a poster or any other presentation method you like.
2   Decide on which market you wish to investigate, for example, soft drinks, health and beauty, sports, and so on.
3   After some initial research, choose which organisation you wish to investigate in more depth.
4   Using the internet, quality newspapers or your own knowledge, research and write about each PESTEC factor in relation to your chosen organisation.

Important! Don't just describe an example of the factor; make sure you explain how each one *impacts*, positively or negatively, on your organisation.

Quick questions 1.5 ?

1   Identify three different tax changes that can impact on organisations.
2   Compare fiscal and monetary policy.
3   Outline two social and two technological changes in recent years.
4   Describe one positive and one negative impact of competition on an organisation.
5   Identify three stages of the economic cycle and outline the impact on sales.

Key question 1.3 ?

Explain the impact of two external factors on a large organisation.

Now, go to page 52 and try the exam-style questions practice – Chapter 1: Set 1.

Topic 6
Internal factors

What you should know

Impact of and how to overcome the following internal factors:
★ Finance
★ Staff
★ Technology
★ Corporate culture

Factors and their impact

Internal factors are the different situations that impact on the success of an organisation which arise from *inside* the organisation. Organisations are able to control internal factors.

Finance

All organisations need finance in order to achieve their objectives. The following are possible situations that may arise due to **budget constraints** and **no availability of finance** to rectify the situation:
- The organisation may not be able to implement decisions and take the courses of action it wishes to, such as:
  - expanding the business by developing new products
  - offering wage rises to motivate staff.
- The organisation may have to take drastic action to cut costs, such as:
  - making staff redundancies (downsizing)
  - removing a layer of management (delayering).

Staff

Managers can impact on an organisation in the following ways:
1 **Level of risk** – sometimes managers go for the 'safe' option which won't necessarily meet the objectives of the business, such as maximising profits. On the other hand, some managers take too much risk and, when things go wrong, put an organisation into financial difficulties.
2 **Experience and expertise** – a good manager can lead and motivate a team to success, while a bad manager can cause low morale, a high turnover of staff and a drop in productivity.

Employees can impact on an organisation in the following ways:
1 **Training** – a well-trained employee fulfils their role efficiently and is an asset to the company; a badly trained one can be incapable of performing basic functions, such as interacting with customers, and is detrimental to the organisation.
2 **Morale** – employee morale needs to be high as, if morale is low, it could impact on the performance levels of staff, increase staff absenteeism or worse, lead to industrial action such as a strike.

Remember

'Staff' refers to both employees and managers and both can impact on the success of a business.

3 **Experience** – employees need to have experience of doing the job in order to develop the skills and expertise to carry out their jobs effectively.

4 **Capacity** – a business will not be able to perform to its best if it is not fully staffed. Sometimes when a business tries to recruit more staff, labour shortages can prevent success. An example is the lack of teachers of certain subjects.

Technology

An organisation's existing technology must be modern and fit for twenty-first-century business. If it is not, the organisation will be left behind by its competitors. Ways in which existing technology can impact on a business include the following:

- **Breakdowns can be catastrophic**, examples include a contact centre losing Wi-Fi connection and so being unable to serve customers, or machines in a factory breaking down and production coming to a halt.
- **Loss of relationships** can impact negatively on employee morale and rapport as staff email each other more rather than having face-to-face conversations.
- **Lack of technology** can leave the organisation behind its competitors, for example not selling online (e-commerce) means a business is missing out on a global market it can sell to 24/7.
- **Financial cost** of installing and replacing technology (most modern technology has a very short life cycle).
- **Staff need to be trained** in how to use new technology or new versions of existing technology.

Corporate culture

Corporate culture is the set of values, beliefs and customs that is shared by all people in an organisation. Methods used to promote corporate culture include:

- **Company values** – These need to be developed by the founder as values are hard to 'adopt' years down the line. Examples include having a strong corporate social responsibility (CSR) policy. This can be outlined to stakeholders through a mission statement.
- **Office layout** – An open-plan office layout can encourage a relaxed atmosphere in an organisation. It can also encourage better communication and idea sharing among staff. Some modern technology companies such as Facebook and Google have very relaxed office environments that include free cafés, sofas and beanbags for staff to sit on, and even sleep pods for staff to have a nap at work!
- **Corporate colours** – Corporate colours give organisations and their staff a strong corporate identity. A good example of this is easyJet's

Figure 1.17 Facebook has a bright, fun and quirky office environment

'orange' culture. Uniforms, planes, hotels and even their offices are bedecked in their famous orange colour! Colours also help customers recognise the organisation easily. Also, while **uniform** can be seen as part of a culture so can a **casual dress code** as it can be seen to relax staff and make them more productive.

- **Uniformity of layout** – Ever been to a McDonald's abroad? Exactly the same as in the UK, isn't it? Uniformity of premises such as offices, shops and restaurants makes it easier for staff to transfer between branches and encourages customers to feel at ease, no matter what branch they are in.

- **Language and jargon** – An organisation can invent its own quirky words and phrases that help give employees a sense of belonging and appeal to customers looking to buy from a business that is a bit different. For example, Disneyland theme parks call their staff 'actors' and their customers 'the audience', and innocent, the smoothie brand, has a very original approach to the language on its packaging. They say 'We've always written and talked to our drinkers in the same way we talk to each other, our mums and the local shopkeeper. We say hello, we're friendly and we try to be interesting. Our tone of voice is the bedrock of the brand. We were chatting away on our packaging long before banks and bags of salad started trying to be your best friend. Which is why we've grown into a brand that's known for being genuine, and we're very careful to keep it that way.'

- **Symbols, slogans and mottos** – The use of brand logos help give organisations identity that both customers and staff easily recognise. Also, the use of slogans and mottos can help reinforce business objectives to staff. For example, Honda's motto 'The Power of Dreams' sums up to designers and production staff that they are a forward-thinking business that designs and produces cutting-edge products for customers.

- **Rituals** – Some UK organisations have 'dress-down Fridays' to help relax their staff and break down the barriers that uniforms or office attire can create. Some American businesses have Friday afternoon barbecues for employees to get together and chat informally. Some Japanese companies even meet together in the morning to exercise and chant company songs. Similarly, Southwest Airlines' cabin crew sing the safety instructions and their pilots tell jokes over the intercom!

- **Stories** – Stories of past important events in an organisation's life can help new staff become familiar with the expectations and direction of the organisation. For example, at Procter & Gamble legend has it that one of their staff members was out shopping and saw an entire shelf of one of their products that was faulty. To save the company embarrassment he bought the shop's entire stock of the product. He was, of course, reimbursed by P&G and applauded for his commitment to ensuring good **quality** (see Topic 19) in the business.

- **Reward culture** – Many employees respond well to financial incentives such as bonuses, commission and pay rises. Others like the recognition and status of 'employee of the month' awards and promotions.

- **Flexible working arrangements** – An organisation can utilise flexible working arrangements such as flexitime or working from home. This can create a culture of trust and empowerment.

Figure 1.18 'easyJet orange' is instantly recognisable

Figure 1.19 innocent packaging showing its quirky culture

Remember

Real examples of corporate culture are a great way to remember all the different ways a business can develop a positive culture.

Case study 1.9
Facebook

Most people are aware of the culture at large technology companies such as Google and Facebook from movies such as *The Internship* and *The Social Network*, which portray some of the aspects of modern office culture. Facebook, like other tech giants, has very appealing office environments with free coffee shops, beanbag and couch seating, games rooms and more! Facebook has a *very* flat organisational structure and employees aren't told what to do. Instead, they are empowered to make their own decisions and start their own projects. There is a very relaxed working environment. Employees can wear casual clothes and start and finish when they want, to suit the employee's own preferences. Jobs at Facebook are stressful and some employees work better after a long lie-in and work late into the evening. They can work from home, in one of the comfortable areas in the office, in 'third spaces' nearby or at their desk.

Discussion points

In pairs, groups or on your own, consider:

1 What elements of Facebook's corporate culture are evident in the example above?
2 What will be the advantages of Facebook's culture for:
 • employees
 • management?
3 Which elements of Facebook's culture would you like/dislike when you get a job and why?

Table 1.27 Advantages and disadvantages of strong corporate culture

Advantages	Disadvantages
Flexible working arrangements mean staff work when and where they are most productive.	Culture is hard to introduce unless it starts from the founders.
Employees feel part of the organisation through the use of uniforms, jargon, and so on.	Staff have to be made aware of changes to culture and if they aren't they may resist change.
Customers gain a sense of a quality product/service.	Modern office cultures can leave some employees physically and socially distant from others, demotivating them.
Rituals create a relaxed ethos and can improve employee relations.	Some cultures can be seen as a 'bribe' to get staff on board.
Employee loyalty is increased as they are happy in their jobs and feel a sense of belonging to the business.	Management can lose focus and control if a culture is too 'loose'.
High-quality new staff are attracted to the business as they like the idea of working in the culture.	
A relaxed working environment, empowerment and a flat hierarchy can motivate staff.	

Quick questions 1.6

1 Describe ways in which managers and employees can impact an organisation.
2 Describe the impact of a lack of staff.
3 Outline two ways in which existing technology can negatively impact a business.
4 Describe the term 'corporate culture'.
5 Outline three methods of developing a corporate culture.

Key question 1.4

Explain the impact of two internal factors on a large organisation.

Topic 7
Stakeholders

What you should know

★ Conflicts of interest ★ Interdependence

Stakeholder – interests and influence

A **stakeholder** is an individual or group of people who have an interest in the success of an organisation. **Internal stakeholders** are from *within* the organisation, such as owners (or shareholders), managers and employees. **External stakeholders** are from *outside* the organisation, such as government, banks, customers, suppliers, pressure groups and HMRC (the government organisation responsible for collecting taxes).

Table 1.28 outlines the **interest** and **influence** of selected stakeholders.

> **Hints & tips** ★
>
> Interest and Influence are both N5 topics rather than Higher topics. However, it may be useful to understand them both for a number of stakeholders to help tackle the Higher level stakeholder topics.

Table 1.28 The interest and influences of selected stakeholders on businesses

Stakeholder	Interest	Influence
Owners	Profits in order to see a return on their investment.	Can invest more money. Can make important decisions.
Managers	May be given bonuses, pay rises or promotions based on the organisation's performance.	Can make decisions.
Employees	Want job security and perhaps a pay rise.	Can affect standard of work. Can take industrial action.
Customers	Demand a quality product/service and value for money.	Can take their custom elsewhere. Can spread good/bad word to others.
Suppliers	Want continued business and the business to pay its debts.	Can change prices. Can adjust the quality of supplies. Can change account terms.

Conflict of interest

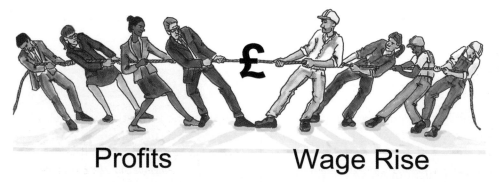

Profits   Wage Rise

Figure 1.20 Sometimes two stakeholder groups can't both get what they want

Although all stakeholders want a business to succeed, they can often conflict in their individual aims. In other words, two stakeholders both cannot get what they want at the same time. Some examples of **conflict of interest** are given in Table 1.29:

> **Hints & tips** ★
>
> A common mistake by students is assuming a competitor is a stakeholder. Competitors are **not** stakeholders, as they don't wish the organisation to **succeed**, which is the definition of a stakeholder.

Table 1.29 Examples of conflicts of interest

Conflicting stakeholders	Conflict example
Employees vs owners/managers	Employees want a pay rise, whereas owners want to maximise profits. *If employees get a pay rise it will lower the amount of profits the owner will receive.*
Customers vs owners/managers	Customers want low prices and value for money, whereas owners want to raise prices to maximise profits and meet their own objectives. *Low prices and high prices can't both happen! So businesses and customers 'meet in the middle', known as the **equilibrium price**.*
Suppliers vs owners/managers	Suppliers want to be paid as soon as possible ideally in cash, whereas the owners want trade credit to keep good cash flow in the business. *Suppliers and owners can also disagree on the prices of products, discounts, quality of supplies, delivery time and so on.*
Government vs owners/managers	Governments may want to introduce legislation to improve society; however, owners may disagree with the legislation as it will impact negatively on their business. *For example, the government raising the minimum wage will lower the profits of a business as wage costs will increase.*

Interdependence of stakeholders

Stakeholders need to work together if the business is to succeed. Some stakeholder groups rely on others to help them achieve their interests.

This is known as the **interdependence of stakeholders**. Some examples of interdependence are given in Table 1.30:

Remember

Stakeholders and shareholders are not the same thing. (A common mistake!) A shareholder is one example of stakeholder.

Table 1.30 The interdependence of stakeholders

Interdependent stakeholders	Interdependent example
Owners/managers and governments	Owners/managers need governments to make good decisions, such as lowering taxes to improve the spending power of customers and therefore sales, while governments need owners to create jobs.
Owners/managers and suppliers	Managers need suppliers to provide quality raw materials to improve the quality of the finished product, while suppliers need managers to keep buying from them and keep them in business.
Owners/managers and customers	Owners need customers to buy their products and customers need a good quality of product and customer service from the owners of the business.
Owners and employees	Owners need employees to perform their best to increase sales and profits through work rate or customer service, while employees need owners to make good decisions to keep the business profitable and their jobs safe.
Managers and employees	Employees and managers need to work together to help the business to succeed in order to keep their jobs secure.

Quick questions 1.7

1 Describe the term 'stakeholder'.
2 Describe what is meant by a conflict of interest.
3 Describe the interests HMRC has in an organisation.
4 Describe the influence of customers on an organisation.
5 Describe the interdependence of owners and governments.

Key question 1.5

Describe two conflicts of interest that could exist between stakeholders.

Hints & tips

The 'business' is **not** a stakeholder. Students often make this mistake of comparing 'the business' with another stakeholder in terms of interdependence or conflict. This will attract 0 marks in an exam question.

Structures

What you should know

Features of the following structures:

★ Tall and flat
★ Centralised and decentralised
★ Matrix structure
★ Entrepreneurial structure

Features of staff groupings:

★ The effect of downsizing
★ The effect of delayering

Management structures

Organisations are known as organisations because they are, well, *organised*! Each organisation can use a variety of different methods to organise and group its staff and resources in a way that suits it best. One way in which they can do this is through the main **structure** of the organisation.

Tall structure

Most organisations have a **hierarchy**. This means positions within the organisation with different levels of authority and responsibility; those with the least amount of authority and responsibility at the bottom of the organisation and those with the most at the top. Commands flow down from the decision-makers at the top of the organisation to the workers at the bottom. This is known as the **chain of command**. A tall structure has many levels of management and resembles a large pyramid. This type of structure suits large organisations with many specialised departments.

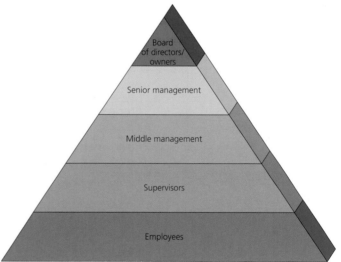

Figure 1.21 There are many levels of management and a long chain of command in a tall structure

Table 1.31 Advantages and disadvantages of a tall structure

Advantages	Disadvantages
Each staff member knows their role and who to report to.	Communications take time to flow down through the levels, which slows down decision-making.
With many levels come many promotion opportunities which can motivate staff.	The organisation can be slow to react to changes in the market.
There is a **narrow span of control** which means: ● managers have more time for planning, supervision and decision-making ● managers can support subordinates.	The **narrow span of control** means: ● managers supervise work more closely, which can put staff under pressure ● managers have fewer staff to share ideas with.

Flat structure

A **flat structure** is also a pyramid-shaped structure and, like a tall structure, commands flow from top to bottom. However, a flat structure has fewer levels of management and a shorter chain of command than a tall structure. This type of structure suits small- to medium-sized organisations.

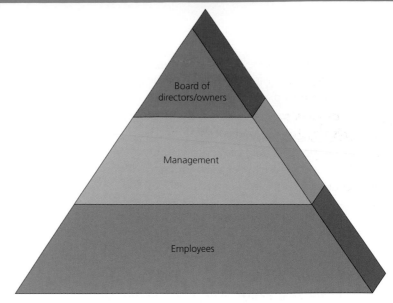

Figure 1.22 There are fewer management levels and a shorter chain of command in a flat structure

Table 1.32 Advantages and disadvantages of a flat structure

Advantages	Disadvantages
Information can be communicated quickly between levels.	Fewer levels means fewer promotion opportunities so quality staff may leave to gain promotion in larger organisations.
The organisation can respond quickly to external (PESTEC) factors, such as competition.	As there are fewer management levels, staff may be delegated more tasks, which could put them under pressure.
There is a **wide span of control** which means: ● managers have to delegate tasks to staff which can raise morale as staff feel trusted ● staff are empowered to make decisions themselves.	The **wide span of control** means: ● managers' time is at a premium which can lead to snap decisions ● less time for planning ● subordinates may have no one to seek help from.

Delayering

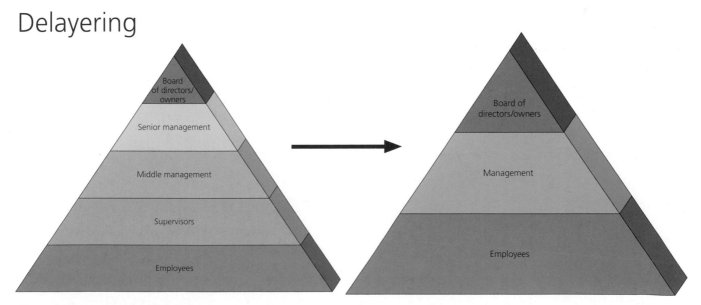

Figure 1.23 An example of delayering

Removing one or more levels of management from a tall structure, to make it *flatter*, is known as **delayering**.

Table 1.33 Advantages and disadvantages of delayering

Advantages	Disadvantages
Money is saved on paying the salaries of the management level that is removed.	There are fewer promotion opportunities for staff.
Quicker decision-making and communication are possible as there is a shorter chain of command.	Redundancy payments will cost the organisation a significant amount of money.
The organisation can be more responsive to changes in the market as there are fewer levels for information to pass through up to the decision-makers.	The organisation will lose key members of staff in the restructure.
There is a wider span of control (see Table 1.32).	There is a wider span of control (see Table 1.32).

Hints & tips

Use these key terms when discussing structures:

✓ **Chain of command:** *The flowing of information and decisions through an organisation.*

✓ **Superior:** *Someone of a higher rank in the organisation.*

✓ **Subordinate:** *Someone of a lower rank in the organisation*

✓ **Line relationship:** *The relationship between a superior and a subordinate.*

✓ **Authority:** *The power to make decisions and to command subordinates.*

✓ **Delegate:** *To pass management tasks on to subordinates.*

✓ **Span of control:** *The number of subordinates working under a superior.*

✓ **Empowerment:** *Staff being given decision-making power.*

Activity 1.4

1 On your own or in pairs, draw out the structure of your school or college in the form of an organisation chart.

2 Annotate the chart with the key terms listed above such as span of control, chain of command, lateral relationship, and so on.

Centralised structure

Decision-making and control is kept at the very top level of a **centralised** organisation. In organisations with many branches this means important decision-making being retained within head office and the senior management, directors or owners that work there.

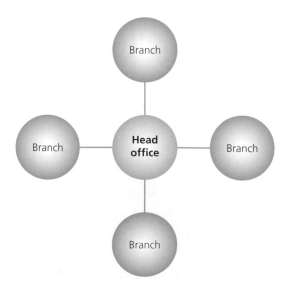

Figure 1.24 In a centralised organisation, control is kept in the centre at the very top level

Table 1.34 Advantages and disadvantages of a centralised structure

Advantages	Disadvantages
A high degree of corporate identity and strategy exists as decisions are made for the whole organisation.	Less responsibility is given to subordinates which can result in demotivated staff.
Procedures are standardised which ensures consistency.	Decisions will not reflect the needs of local markets.
There is low risk of important information leaking from branches or departments.	The organisation will react slowly to external (PESTEC) factors, such as the competition improving their product range.

Decentralised structure

Decision-making and control is delegated to individual branches or departments in decentralised organisations. This type of structure is best used in retail chains that need to respond to the needs of their local markets, such as supermarkets. While the overall strategy of an organisation such as Tesco will still be centralised, many decisions will be decentralised, such as buying and selling local products and advertising in the local area.

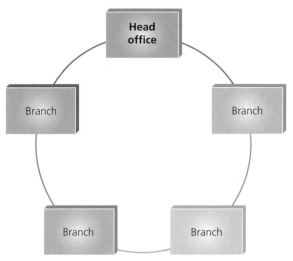

Figure 1.25 In a decentralised organisation, some control is delegated to branches

Table 1.35 Advantages and disadvantages of a decentralised structure

Advantages	Disadvantages
The business reacts quickly to changing external (PESTEC) factors.	The organisation can lose an overall corporate image if each department/branch is operating differently.
Decisions are made quickly as local managers don't need to consult senior managers before implementing decisions.	Local branches could start to compete with each other if they are allowed to make key decisions.
More subordinates are empowered which encourages creativity.	Additional training required for middle management.
Senior management at head office are relieved of the burden of constant decision-making.	Lower-level management can make decisions that could harm the business as a whole.

Matrix structure

A matrix structure involves an organisation being arranged into temporary project teams to carry out a particular task, such as developing a new product or service, or a large-scale construction operation. Teams are made up of employees from different functional areas: marketing, finance, operations, R&D, and so on. Each staff member will have two managers: one will be the manager of their functional area, such as marketing or finance, and the other will be their project manager.

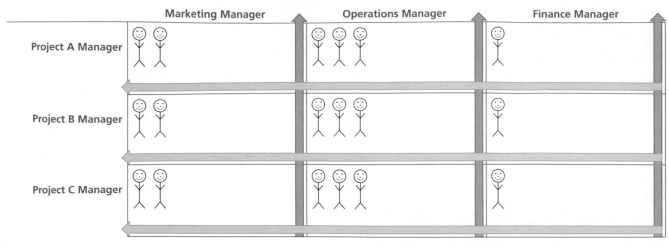

Figure 1.26 Employees report to two managers in a matrix structure

Table 1.36 Advantages and disadvantages of a matrix structure

Advantages	Disadvantages
Each team has specialised staff from all functional areas.	Many managers across all project teams will mean high wage costs.
Complex problems can be solved.	Duplication of resources such as administration staff and equipment.
Staff can use their expertise and as such have job satisfaction and motivation.	Staff can be confused as to who to report to.

Entrepreneurial structure

This is a structure used primarily by small organisations. Usually they have one main decision-maker, the owner himself or herself. Of course, other staff can have some input but generally they are rarely consulted and final decisions are made by the owner.

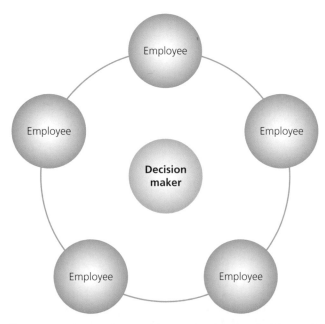

Figure 1.27 An entrepreneurial structure, showing decision-making at the core of the organisation

Table 1.37 Advantages and disadvantages of an entrepreneurial structure

Advantages	Disadvantages
Decisions are made quickly as there is little consultation.	This structure can create a heavy workload for the main decision maker.
Staff know who they need to report to.	If the owner is busy or not available, key decisions can't be made.
High-quality decisions are made as decision-makers are experienced.	Other staff don't get a chance to show initiative, stifling creativity and possibly demotivating some staff.

Organisational groupings

As well as using a **management structure** such as tall, flat or entrepreneurial, an organisation can structure itself through the use of **groupings**.

Functional grouping

This involves grouping an organisation into departments called functional areas, based on skills and expertise. The main functional areas of most organisations are marketing, finance, operations and human resources. These main functional areas can be supported by administration and IT departments. Very small organisations do not have sufficient staff resources to be able to group their staff in this way.

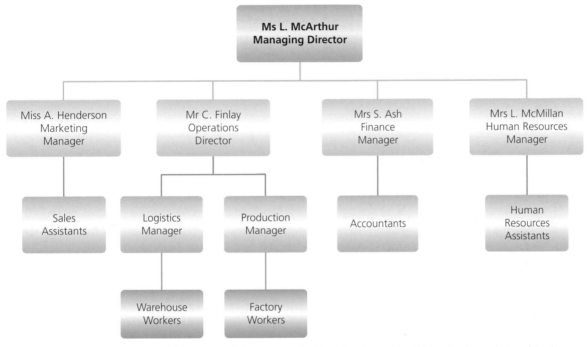

Figure 1.28 An organisation is split into specialist areas in the functional grouping. Note the line relationships between subordinates and superiors – this illustrates chain of command

Table 1.38 Advantages and disadvantages of functional grouping

Advantages	Disadvantages
Staff with similar skills and expertise are together, allowing for specialisation, i.e. each department becomes excellent at what it does.	The organisation can become too large to manage if functional departments grow rapidly.
Staff know who to report to and can get guidance from more experienced staff in their area of expertise.	Functional grouping is often coupled with a centralised structure so communication can take a while to filter through to functional departments, causing slow reactions to external (PESTEC) factors.
Clear structure, lines of authority and career paths are mapped out for employees.	Functional departments can be more interested in their own objectives rather than the organisation's objectives as a whole.

Location grouping

This is grouping an organisation into geographical divisions. Each division will operate to serve customers in a particular location. Large organisations, such as multinational businesses, might have a Glasgow office, a London office and a San Francisco office, for example.

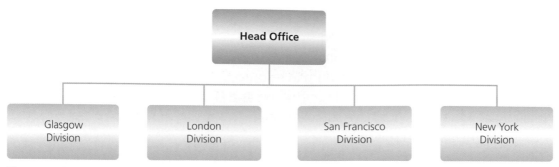

Figure 1.29 Location/geographical grouping

Table 1.39 Advantages and disadvantages of location grouping

Advantages	Disadvantages
Each division can meet the needs of its local market, e.g. different tastes or fashions in different areas or countries.	Duplication of resources, such as administration staff or computer equipment, across each group is inefficient.
The business can react to changing external (PESTEC) factors quickly.	Divisions may compete against each other and forget the overall objectives of the organisation as a whole.
It is easy to identify a failing 'area' and hold regional managers accountable.	Local knowledge and relationships with local customers are lost if staff leave.

Hints & tips ⭐

Most organisations have both a management structure and a grouping. Figure 1.29 is a diagram of the location grouping and also an example of a centralised structure. Look at the product/service grouping diagram (Figure 1.30). It is also an example of a centralised structure.

Product/service grouping

This is grouping an organisation into divisions that deal with different products or services. This is suitable for large conglomerate organisations such as P&G or Virgin. Virgin, for example, has different groups for Virgin Money, Virgin Atlantic, Virgin Media, etc.

Table 1.40 Advantages and disadvantages of product/service grouping

Advantages	Disadvantages
The business can react to changing external (PESTEC) factors that affect each particular group's market quickly.	Duplication of resources can occur.
It is easy for management to identify struggling products/services.	A new group needs to be set up every time the business launches a new product – meaning more staff, equipment and premises costs.

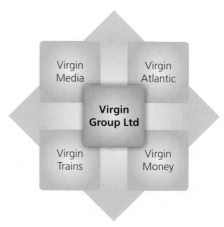

Figure 1.30 Virgin grouping

Technology grouping

This is similar to a product/service grouping but involves businesses organising their activities according to the technology or production processes used.

Table 1.41 Advantages and disadvantages of technology grouping

Advantages	Disadvantages
High degree of specialisation can occur in production.	High degree of specialised training is required.
Problems in the production process can be easily identified.	Only an option for very large businesses with different production processes.
Capital intensive – which can reduce wage costs.	Capital intensive – which is expensive.

Customer grouping

This involves grouping the organisation's resources into divisions that each deal with a different type of customer. For example, a business might have a division for retail customers, wholesale customers and online customers.

Figure 1.31 Customer grouping

Select a business of your choice or ask your teacher to suggest one.
- Research the business's website to find out how staff are grouped (often you can find this out in the 'working for us' section).
- Design a diagram (see Figure 1.30 for an example) to illustrate the grouping.
- Add this diagram to your notes to supplement them or create a colourful poster!

Table 1.42 Advantages and disadvantages of customer grouping

Advantages	Disadvantages
Each group can tailor its product or service to its own type of customer.	Duplication of resources can occur.
Customer loyalty can build up due to the high level of personal service that can be achieved.	This is only suitable for large businesses, with many customer types/segments that are of sufficient size. It is inefficient to offer a group for a small customer segment.

Downsizing

This involves an organisation either closing an unprofitable division, such as a location group, altogether or merging two divisions together.

Table 1.43 Advantages and disadvantages of downsizing

Advantages	Disadvantages
This can cut the costs of wages and rent.	Valuable skills and knowledge are lost when redundancies are made.
The business is 'leaner' (more efficient) and can become more competitive.	Remaining staff feel vulnerable and are demotivated.

Remember

There is lots of cross-over between groupings. For example, notice that **most** groupings have 'duplication of resources' as a disadvantage. Another point that can be applied to all groups is that '**groups compete**' with each other. For all but the Functional grouping it is **easy to identify which group is poorly performing**. You would only be credited for this knowledge once in the exam but it should help when revising.

Quick questions 1.8

1 Describe the term 'chain of command'.
2 Compare a tall management structure with a flat management structure.
3 Describe the following terms:
   a) delayering
   b) downsizing.
4 Outline two advantages of a narrow span of control.
5 Outline the use of grouping staff by function.

Key questions 1.6

1 **Describe** two internal structures (management structures or groupings) that a business could use.
2 **Justify** the use of the structures you described above.

Topic 9
Decision-making

What you should know

★ Types of decisions
★ Factors affecting decisions
★ Measuring success of decisions
★ SWOT analysis
★ Role of a manager

Types of decisions

There are three different types of decisions, strategic, tactical and operational, as illustrated in Table 1.44:

Table 1.44 Three types of decisions: strategic, tactical and operational

Type of decision	Length of decision	Decision-maker	Purpose	Risk
Strategic	Long term	Senior managers	To meet the overall purpose and direction of the organisation, e.g. to grow the business.	High
Tactical	Medium term	Middle managers	To achieve the strategic decisions, e.g. launch new products to grow organically.	Medium
Operational	Short term, day to day	Supervisors/all staff	To react to situations as they arise, e.g. dealing with a customer complaint.	Low

Centralised and decentralised decision-making

- In a **centralised** structure (see pages 40–1) the decision-making is kept at the senior level of the business. For example, fast food franchises don't let their franchisees make any major decisions on prices or promotions so they retain an overall consistency and identity.
- In a **decentralised** structure (see page 41) decision-making is delegated to branches or outlets. For example, Waterstones operates in this way and lets branch managers order books that reflect the local area and what local customers would want to read.

SWOT analysis

An organisation can use a structured decision-making model known as a **SWOT analysis**. This allows it to look at its internal (*inside* the organisation) strengths and weaknesses, as well as external (*outside* the organisation) opportunities and threats. A SWOT analysis is often laid out in a grid (see Figure 1.32) for easy comparison of the organisation's position and to allow an informed decision to be made about future actions.

Strengths

Strengths are things the organisation is good at. These could be:
- availability of finance
- well-known brands or products
- goods/services that make the most profits
- products that are 'benchmarks' in the market which competitors try to copy
- assets the business owns, such as a large modern factory, modern technology or a retail outlet in a prime location
- high-quality staff and good staff morale.

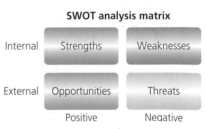

Figure 1.32 SWOT analysis matrix

Weaknesses

Weaknesses are things the organisation is ineffective at. These could be:

- lack of finance
- lack of technology
- poor customer service reputation
- faulty products
- products or branches that are making losses
- assets that are in a state of disrepair, such as a crumbling factory or ageing fleet
- untrained staff or low staff morale.

Opportunities

Opportunities are the possible chances a business could take that arise due to something happening outside the organisation's control. These might be:

- a competitor going bust, so the business could take on its customers
- a boom period in the economy that the business could exploit
- customer tastes and fashions falling in line with an organisation's specialism
- governments introducing favourable legislation
- advancements in technology that the business could exploit, for example, e-commerce.

Threats

Threats are things that might impact on a business achieving its aims or making positive decisions. These may be:

- competitors' actions, such as cheaper prices or better-quality products
- a downturn in the economy, such as a recession
- customer tastes and fashions changing, away from those the business specialises in
- governments introducing legislation that impacts badly on the organisation
- advancements in technology that could leave the business behind its rivals.

Table 1.45 Advantages and disadvantages of using SWOT analysis

Advantages of using SWOT	Disadvantages of using SWOT
Identifies strengths and allows a business to build upon them.	A SWOT analysis is very time consuming, which can slow down decision-making.
Identifies weaknesses and allows them to be addressed.	A SWOT analysis is a very structured process which can stifle creativity and gut reactions from managers.
Identifies opportunities and allows them to be exploited.	A SWOT analysis can generate many ideas; however, it doesn't help pick the correct one.
Identifies threats and allows them to be turned into opportunities, e.g. embracing advancing technology, not allowing it to leave the business behind.	A SWOT analysis produces a result that reflects the opinions of those who carry it out which could lead to bias.
Time is taken to analyse the business's current position so no rash decisions are made.	A SWOT analysis considers information that is available at a particular moment and may become outdated quickly.

Activity 1.6

Activity 1.6

On your own or in pairs, carry out your own SWOT analysis on an organisation of your choice.

1 Copy the SWOT diagram in Figure 1.32; you can do this either on paper or using a table in Microsoft Word.
2 Using the internet, newspapers or your own knowledge, find out information for each section and complete your diagram.

Factors affecting the quality of decisions

Organisations often face a variety of issues when making decisions. There are many internal factors that can affect the quality of decision-making.

Human resources

The human resources, people within the organisation, can affect decision-making in the following ways:
- managers' ability, training and experience to make good decisions
- how much risk the managers will take when making decisions
- staff resistance to change
- managers' ability to handle stressful and complex situations
- the likelihood of overpowering managing directors or owners overturning decisions made by middle management.

Hints & tips

You can refer to the four 'internal factors' here, as long as they are used in context, i.e. of making quality decisions.

Availability of finance

Whether or not the organisation has or can get hold of finance can impact on decision-making in the following ways:
- whether finance is available to exploit the opportunities, address weaknesses or build on strengths
- financial constraints may mean an organisation cannot choose the best solution to a problem.

Technology

The availability of technology to help make informed decisions can affect the quality of decisions, for example:
- **Spreadsheets** can improve the accuracy of calculations using formula and perform 'What if?' statements to calculate the projected outcome of a decision.
- **Databases** can improve the speed of decision-making by making it easy to search for information quickly using queries and sort functions.
- **Email** can be used to communicate information regarding decisions to many employees at once and attachments containing information can be sent which reduces printing costs.
- **Internet** sites can be used to find out a vast amount of information to make an informed decision.

- **Video-conferencing** (also known as tele-conferencing or simply video-calling) can reduce the need for managers to travel to meetings, saving time and travel **costs**, but allowing key players to have a hand in decisions.

Other factors

- Company policy may restrict the decisions made or the options that are available to decision-makers.
- Lack of opportunity to consult others may mean that decisions are poor and staff resist change.

Figure 1.33 A management meeting using video-conferencing

- Time constraints can restrict the time taken to decide on a course of action or to implement a final decision.
- The quality of the information available on which to base the decision may be poor. In other words it could be out of date, biased, not relevant or incomplete, for example.

Role of a manager

The roles of a manager have developed over the years. The main roles are based on the work of business management theorist, Henri Fayol. He outlined the five functions of management.

- **Plan** – The function of management is to be looking ahead, seeing potential opportunities, or problems, setting targets and strategies. The importance of planning can be remembered by the phrase: 'If you fail to plan, you plan to fail!'
- **Organise** – Management must set tasks for other employees that need to be carried out to achieve set targets.
- **Command** – Managers should issue instructions to employees.
- **Co-ordinate** – Management must bring together the resources of the business to achieve the overall objectives that have been set.
- **Control** – Managers need to ensure they are measuring and correcting the activities of the organisation. A manager looks at what is being done and checks this against what was expected.

Modern-day roles

Since Henri Fayol outlined the five functions of management, managers have adopted more modern roles. Nowadays, in addition to the five functions that Fayol identified, managers must:

- **Delegate** – give subordinates the authority to carry out management-level tasks. This helps lessen the manager's workload and achieve the next role.
- **Motivate** – give his team a reason to enjoy their work. Workers are motivated in different ways (see Topic 23).

Remember

... the role of a manager with the mnemonic POCCC-DM.

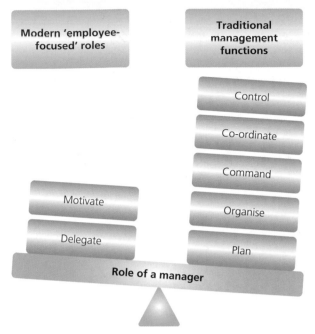

Figure 1.34 The role of the manager

Assessing the effectiveness of a decision

Managers will assess the effectiveness of a decision in the following ways:
- Measuring sales levels to see if they have increased
- Analysing profit levels to see if they have improved
- Interviewing staff to assess their opinion of the decision
- Monitoring staff morale, absence and turnover following major decisions
- Finding out from customers about improvements in service
- Tracking changes in share prices to major decisions
- Researching customer review sites or social media feedback

Quick questions 1.9

1 Describe what is meant by a 'tactical decision' and give an example.
2 Outline three ways to analyse the effectiveness of a decision.
3 Justify the use of a SWOT analysis.
4 Suggest three possible threats to an organisation achieving success.
5 Describe what is meant by centralised decision-making.

Hints & tips

Be prepared to answer questions in context, e.g. the role of a manager in **decision-making** or the role of a **finance** manager, as well as the general roles/functions of a manager as described here.

Remember

... to follow the **command word** in each exam question! This is usually the first word in the question and *commands* you how you should structure your answer.

Exam-style questions practice – Chapter 1: Set 1

1. Compare the features of a public limited company (PLC) with those of a private limited company (Ltd). **(3 marks)**
2. Describe the advantages of setting up an organisation as a social enterprise. **(3 marks)**
3. Discuss the use of franchising for the franchiser. **(4 marks)**
4. Describe the features of a multinational organisation. **(3 marks)**
5. Explain methods of internal (organic) growth an organisation can use. **(5 marks)**
6. Discuss the use of outsourcing. **(6 marks)**
7. Discuss ways of achieving growth. **(4 marks)**
8. Distinguish between a decentralised management structure and a centralised management structure. **(3 marks)**
9. Explain economic factors that can affect an organisation. **(5 marks)**
10. Describe the ways in which competition policy can affect an organisation. **(4 marks)**

Exam-style questions practice – Chapter 1: Set 2

1. Explain the benefits to an organisation of having a strong corporate culture. **(5 marks)**
2. Describe factors that affect quality decisions being made. **(4 marks)**
3. Explain the benefits of the matrix structure. **(3 marks)**
4. Explain the advantages and disadvantages of grouping by location. **(4 marks)**
5. Compare the use of customer grouping with product grouping. **(4 marks)**
6. Distinguish between strategic and operational decisions. **(3 marks)**
7. Discuss the use of a structured decision-making model, such as SWOT analysis. **(5 marks)**
8. Describe the role of a manager in an organisation. **(5 marks)**
9. Explain the advantages of using technology to aid decision-making. **(4 marks)**
10. Explain the costs of downsizing to an organisation. **(3 marks)**

What you should know

★ Market led vs product led
★ Consumer behaviours

Customers – their wants and needs

It is the role of the Marketing department to anticipate, identify and satisfy the needs and wants of customers.

Marketing aims to raise customer awareness of their products. The level to which they try and meet the needs of customers will depend on whether the business is **market led** or **product led**.

Market or product led?

Table 2.1 Characteristics of market-led and product-led businesses

Market led	Product led
The business develops products based on customer wants.	The business produces products that it believes customers will want and tries to convince them to buy them.
High levels of market research carried out to determine customer wants.	Market research is not seen as important. There are, however, high levels of product research and development.
Market-led businesses often exist in highly competitive markets.	New technologies, with little to no competition, are often product led.
The marketing mix will be responsive to changes in external factors and consumer behaviour.	Often the product is unresponsive to changing external factors.

Consumer behaviour

Businesses, especially market-led businesses, need to take account of **consumer behaviour**. Consumer behaviour is the thoughts consumers have and the actions they take when purchasing products.

In order to satisfy consumers' needs and wants, the market-led business needs to understand why, what, how and where consumers buy products.

Table 2.2 Understanding consumer behaviour

Consumer behaviour	Description	Impact on market-led business
Why do consumers buy products?	Need/want, social status, gift for someone else?	Businesses need to understand the different motivations customers have and offer products accordingly. This is linked to Maslow's hierarchy (see page 110), i.e. some purchases are for basic needs e.g. food, others are for self-actualisation needs, e.g. a Rolex watch.
What types of purchases do consumers make?	**Routine/habitual** buying, e.g. food or fuel. **Impulse** buying just because it caught their eye? **Informed** purchases, e.g. a new car.	Marketing has to raise awareness of products. Promotion methods, such as sales promotions or advertising, can influence routine purchases. Point of sale merchandising materials, for example displays, can influence impulse buying. Informed purchases require information to be readily available, such as digital brochures, a live chat function on a website or links to review articles and videos.
How do consumers purchase products?	Do consumers pay with: ● cash/debit card ● credit card ● store credit etc.?	A business needs to be responsive to changes in how consumers wish to purchase products, for example, the move to a cashless society and the introduction of contactless card payments is a result of the need for convenience due to lifestyle changes.
Where do consumers purchase products?	Retail outlets? E-commerce? Catalogues?	Businesses need to adapt and sell products in ways that are responsive to changes in consumer behaviour. There has been a massive growth in e-commerce, again due to the need for convenience.

Quick questions 2.1

1 a) Outline two types of consumer behaviour.
   b) Describe the impact on businesses of the behaviour you referred to in question 1a).
2 Describe what is meant by impulse buying.
3 Describe two features of a market-led business.

Topic 11
Market research

What you should know

★ Sampling
★ Field research methods
★ Desk research methods

Market research – the two main types

Market research is essential in order to anticipate and identify customers' needs and wants, especially for market-led businesses. There are two main types of market research, **field research** and **desk research**. Each has advantages and disadvantages:

Table 2.3 Advantages and disadvantages of different types of research

Type of research	Advantages	Disadvantages
Desk research: Involves researching and analysing information that has already been gathered. Methods of desk research include: • competitor's website • online news articles • trade magazines • government publications • financial statements • sales figures • previous market research reports • social media posts/comments • review websites, e.g. Trip Advisor.	Timely – desk information is quick to gather. Cost effective – desk information does not require trained and paid interviewers or research companies. Available – desk information already exists so is easy to look up.	Not objective – desk information is collected and presented by someone else, so could be biased. Not appropriate – desk information is not fit for the *exact* purpose and may have to be 'shoehorned' to fit the business's needs. Not concise – the researcher may have to read through a lot of information to get what is needed.
Field research: Involves gathering brand new information suitable for the business's exact needs. Examples are explored in depth in this chapter.	Complete – field information should have no parts missing. Timely – in the respect that the information is up to date. Appropriate – field information is fit for the purpose it is needed for. Accurate – information should be correct as it can be validated.	Not cost effective – field information requires trained and paid interviewers or expensive research companies.

Field research
Sampling

The total of potential customers of a business's product is known as the **population**. Table 2.4 shows the methods of **sampling**, selecting people from that population to conduct market research on, that can be used.

Table 2.4 Advantages and disadvantages of different types of sampling

Sampling method	Advantages	Disadvantages
Random sampling: The sample is picked randomly, e.g. using a telephone directory or list of customers.	No bias is shown by the researcher. Saves time in selecting the sample.	Sample may not reflect the target market. Can over-represent a certain segment, e.g. all males could be chosen at random. Can be expensive as many calls may have to be made if customer lists are not up to date.
Quota sampling: The researcher chooses from a group of people with certain characteristics.	Quick and easy method as group lists are pre-made. Can select customers that reflect the target market.	The exact sample from each group is not randomised, so researcher bias could be involved.

Remember

... the **value** of research types with the overstuffed TAAACCCO (Timely, Appropriate, Available, Accurate, Concise, Cost effective, Complete, Objective).
Remember this for Section 2 of your assignment too!

Methods of field research

Once a sample population has been identified, the field research method must be chosen.

Hints & tips

*If asked about **methods** of market research you will get 0 marks if you just mention the general costs and benefits of field/desk research. You must go into detail about individual methods, e.g. **hall test** or **competitor websites**.*

Table 2.5 Advantages and disadvantages of different types of field research

Method	Advantages	Disadvantages
Telephone survey: A market researcher telephones customers, usually at home, and asks them questions.	Easy to target specific customers, e.g. calling 0141 numbers to target customers living in Glasgow, to allow local needs to be met. Information is obtained immediately and can be clarified if necessary.	Customers can feel that telephone surveys are intrusive and may not wish to respond. Only short surveys can be carried out.
Postal survey: A survey is sent to customers through the post and is returned once completed.	Easy to target specific customers, e.g. sending out surveys on exclusive products to affluent postcodes, to meet the needs of specific segments. Customers can choose to complete the survey at a time that is most convenient to them.	Questions must be simple and easy to follow for the best result. Customers often view postal surveys as 'junk mail' and will simply ignore them.
Online survey: A website or email is used to ask customers questions.	Customers can be surveyed across a very large geographical area. Online software can often be used to collate and analyse the results easily.	The responses may be too brief to be meaningful, as clarification cannot be gained. Access to the internet must be available.
Personal interview: Often conducted as a street survey or by 'cold calling' at customers' homes.	Allows two-way communication. The interviewer can respond to the customer's body language, tone of voice and facial expression to encourage fuller responses.	It can take a lot of time to conduct the interviews. Customers may feel that this sort of questioning is a nuisance and may not wish to respond.
Hall tests: A product is given to customers to try and their feedback is gathered.	Good-quality feedback can be gathered based on the product trial, allowing changes to be made. Inexpensive and easy to do.	Customers' opinions and feelings can be more difficult to analyse. Customers might feel they need to give a positive response as they have been given a free product.
Focus groups: A group of customers is brought together and asked to answer and discuss questions put forward by a market researcher.	More in-depth feedback can be gathered. Customers have agreed to participate so considered responses are more likely.	Participants are often paid, which can increase R&D (research and development) costs. Strong personalities within the group can sway discussion and opinion.

Method	Advantages	Disadvantages
Consumer audit: Used by large market research companies to continuously monitor customer habits and influences. One means of auditing is to ask some customers to record their responses to products they have purchased.	As the information is gathered over a period of time, customer trends can be identified. More detailed feedback can be gathered on products and so shape future changes.	Participants receive payment so this method can be expensive. Information recorded may be inaccurate or incomplete, and therefore unhelpful.
Test marketing: A new product is launched in a regional area and the reaction is monitored. Successful products are then launched to a wider market.	Changes can be made to products before they are launched to a wider market. Money can be saved on launching a product to a wider market if it is unsuccessful in the test area.	Customers in one area may have tastes that are not representative of the wider market.
Electronic point of sale (EPOS): Information on customer preferences and habits is gathered as their loyalty cards are swiped through electronic tills. Used in conjunction with loyalty schemes to match purchasing information with customer details.	Gathers vital information about consumer behaviour, such as when they buy, what they buy, how they react to promotions or price changes, which can allow an effective marketing mix to be formed and inventory ordered accordingly. Allows retailers to offer promotions, for example, money-off coupons, tailored to the individual customer's actual needs and preferences.	It can be very expensive to set up the systems. It can be time consuming to set up. When used with loyalty schemes, reward points lead to money-off vouchers which lower potential profits for the business. Information can be incomplete if customers decide to shop elsewhere at times.

Quick questions 2.2

1 Describe two methods of sampling.
2 Discuss one advantage and one disadvantage of using EPOS for market research purposes.
3 Suggest three ways to send a survey to customers.
4 Describe what a hall test involves.
5 Outline two disadvantages of using focus groups.

WWW

You will need to use field research methods to complete your coursework assignment. Take a look at: **www.surveymonkey.com**. It's free!

Key question 2.1

Explain two ways market research can be used to enhance the effectiveness of a large organisation.

Hints & tips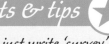

Never just write 'survey' when describing field research. You will gain more marks if you are more specific as to the exact type of survey, e.g. postal, telephone, etc.!

Topic 12
Marketing mix: product

Marketing mix

The marketing mix is the combination of **product**, **price**, **place**, **promotion**, **people**, **process** and **physical evidence** that makes the marketing of a product successful.

Product refers to *what* a business sells. A product can be either a **good** or a **service**.

> ### Remember
>
> It should be easy to remember the marketing mix — they all begin with the letter 'P'. Just remember that at N5 level Business Management you only had to know the '4Ps'; at Higher level you need to know the '7Ps'!

Product life cycle

All products have a life cycle. Some products go through the stages of a life cycle very quickly, known as **fads**, while others can have a life cycle that lasts many decades, for example, Coca-Cola. The stages of the product life cycle are shown in Figure 2.1.

> ### Hints & tips
>
> You need to be able to explain the impact of each stage of the product life cycle on **sales** and **profits**.

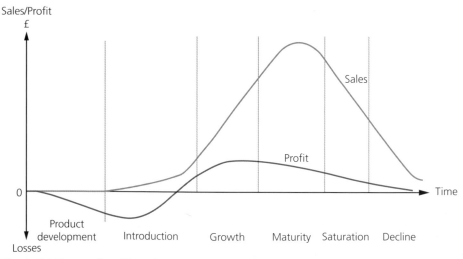

Figure 2.1 The product life cycle

Table 2.6 Stages of the product life cycle and each stage's impact on sales and profits

Stage	Impact on sales	Impact on profits
Research and development (R&D) The product is being researched and developed. Prototypes will be made and tested. Changes may have to be made after research feedback.	There are no sales yet as the product is still being developed.	The product will actually be making a loss due to the costs of development and zero income from sales.
Introduction: The product is launched. This usually coincides with introductory promotional activities to create 'hype' for the product.	Sales are slow to begin with as customers are unsure of the product. Customers may have to be persuaded to move from competitor products.	The product begins to cut into the losses from development, but high promotional costs still result in a loss being made overall.
Growth: The product has been on the market for some time, customers are fully aware of the product and are purchasing it.	Sales start to rise rapidly. This can be the result of slightly reduced prices, lack of competition and/or consumer confidence in the product.	Profits are starting to be made and losses from development and promotions during the initial stages are recouped.
Maturity: The product has been on the market for some time. Competition enters the market.	Sales growth peaks and levels out. Many sales can still be made for a long time at this stage.	Profits can still be healthy but start to fall. The competition will take sales away and thus profits will fall.
Saturation: The product suffers from too many competitors being in the market.	Sales begin to fall as consumers flock to competitors' products.	Profits fall rapidly, especially if prices are slashed to encourage sales.
Decline: The product's life is nearing the end. The product will stop being produced.	Sales fall rapidly and eventually the product will be withdrawn from the market.	Profits continue to fall. Eventually products may be sold at unit cost just to break even.

Activity 2.1

You are going to make your own product life cycle diagram!

1 Choose a business or a market as a whole, for example, you could choose Nintendo or the whole computer consoles market.
2 Create a blank product life cycle diagram by copying the X axis and Y axis of Figure 2.1. You can do this on a poster-sized piece of paper or on a computer using publishing software such as Microsoft Publisher.
3 Research your chosen business or market using the internet, newspapers, magazines, etc. and decide which products belong at each stage. Print or cut out images of these products and stick them along your product life cycle!
4 Add in notes to justify why each product belongs at each stage.
5 Present your findings to others, either via PowerPoint presentation or by describing the features of your poster.

Extension strategies

As sales (and profits) begin to fall as a product matures, a business can attempt to inject new life into the product. This is known as **extending the product life cycle**. There are a number of extension strategies a business can use, which are shown in Table 2.7:

Table 2.7 Product life cycle extension strategies

Extension strategy	Impact
Lowering the price of the product, e.g. through a 'sale'	Reducing prices will make the product more affordable and therefore appeal to more market segments.
Changing the place the product is sold, e.g. selling online	Making the product available in more places will mean it is seen by more potential customers, e.g. using e-commerce will mean a product can be sold worldwide.
Altering the methods of promotion	Changing the way a product is promoted can increase sales simply by raising awareness of that product.
Developing variations of the product, e.g. new flavours	Developing new varieties can mean the product appeals to the tastes and desires of different market segments. Updating the product can utilise the latest technology so make customers want the product again, e.g. annual launches of the latest, updated smartphones.
Rebranding the product	Changing the name of the product can create 'hype'. A new name can appeal to different or wider market segments, e.g. Jif changed to Cif as they found that continental Europeans couldn't pronounce Jif!
Changing the packaging	Redesigning the packaging can make the product appeal to a new market segment, e.g. Harry Potter books also come in a more mature-looking front cover to entice more adults to buy them!
Changing the use of the product	Extending or changing the use of a product can make it appeal to new markets or suit seasonal tastes, e.g. Cadbury's Minirolls were released in ice-cream-inspired flavours and are suitable for freezing, ideal for summer!

Product portfolio

A business should strive to have a product portfolio. This means having a range of products on sale. There are two types of product portfolio: **product line portfolios** and **diversified product portfolios**.

Product line portfolios

A product line portfolio involves having a variety of similar products on sale. Greater profits can be gained from having so many products on sale as different products 'in the line' will appeal to different market segments with different tastes. For example, Arcadia is a clothing company with brands such as Topshop, Topman, Miss Selfridge and Dorothy Perkins; Arcadia can meet the needs of many different market segments such as males, females, young and old.

Diversified product portfolio

A diversified product portfolio involves having products for sale across completely different market segments. This variety spreads the risk across different markets in case one fails. For example, Virgin, which owns Virgin Bank, still had products to fall back on during the banking crisis, such as Virgin Media and Virgin Atlantic.

Case study 2.1

Nestlé

Nestlé has managed to combine an extensive product line with a diversified product portfolio. It is best known for its range of chocolate bars such as KitKat, Aero and Yorkie but it also has a complete range of cereals including Shreddies, Cheerios and Golden Nuggets, as well as a range of other well-known store cupboard staples such as Nescafé, Nesquik and Nestea. It even owns pet food brands such as Purina and Felix!

Figure 2.2 Nestlé's product portfolio

Discussion points

In pairs, groups or on your own:

1 Discuss examples of Nestlé's product line.
2 Discuss examples of Nestlé's diversified product portfolio.
3 Suggest the market segments that different Nestlé products appeal to.

Boston matrix

Businesses can analyse their product portfolio using a **Boston matrix**. This enables products to be analysed on two fronts:

1 **market share** – the percentage of sales in the market a product makes.
2 **market growth** – the overall potential for sales that the market has as a whole.

		Market share	
		High	Low
Market growth	High	Stars	Question marks
	Low	Cash cows	Dogs

Figure 2.3 The Boston matrix

Table 2.8 Boston matrix product types

Product type	Impact
Stars:	
Products that have a high market share in a high-growth market, e.g. Apple's iPad.	Stars need constant investment in marketing to keep ahead in a competitive market.
	Stars allow a business to be a market leader.
	Over time, stars will decline into either question marks or cash cows (see below).
Cash cows:	
Products that have a high market share of a low-growth market, e.g. Microsoft's Office software.	Cash cows should require little marketing expense due to lack of competition.
	Funds generated can be used to further strengthen stars and improve riskier ventures, such as question marks.
Question marks/Problem children:	
Products that have a low market share in a market with high growth potential, e.g. manufacturers of less popular brands of tablet computers.	Question marks can be invested in due to their position in a promising market.
	They need development of a strong marketing mix if they are to be turned into stars.
Dogs:	
Products that have a low market share of a market with low growth, e.g. less popular brands in declining technology industries.	Dogs can adversely affect profits.
	Dogs should be divested due to the lack of market share and the declining market for the product. They cannot be turned into stars.

Advantages and disadvantages of a product portfolio

Table 2.9 Advantages and disadvantages of a product portfolio

Advantages	Disadvantages
Businesses can spread risk over different markets.	There are high costs involved in researching and developing so many products.
A business can meet the needs of different market segments and appeal to more customers.	High marketing costs are incurred to promote so many products.
Newer products can replace those at the end of their life cycle.	Bad publicity surrounding one product can affect the whole portfolio.
A range of products increases the awareness of the brand as a whole.	Resources assigned to new products may affect the performance of existing products.
A business will find it easier to launch new products with a large existing portfolio.	Dogs can drain a business of profits unless they are divested.
Cash cows can fund other, riskier, ventures such as the marketing of stars.	
Stars allow a business to be market leader in one area which will improve the brand image overall.	
Question mark products give businesses an opportunity to invest and grow.	
Dogs can be divested to reduce losses.	

Activity 2.2

You are going to create your own Boston matrix.

1 Choose a business or a market as a whole, for example you could choose Apple or the whole mobile phone market.

2 Create a blank Boston matrix by copying Figure 2.3. You can do this on a poster-sized piece of paper or on a computer using publishing software.

3 Research your chosen company or market using the internet or newspapers and decide which products belong in each box. Print or cut out products and stick them onto your Boston matrix.

4 Add notes justifying why each product belongs in each box.

5 Present your findings to others, either via PowerPoint presentation or by describing the features of your poster.

Quick questions 2.3

1 Outline three extension strategies that could be used to extend a product's life.

2 Describe the following terms:
   a) Market share
   b) Market growth

3 Compare 'star' products with 'cash cows'.

Topic 13
Marketing mix: price

What you should know

★ Pricing strategies
★ Factors affecting pricing strategy

Pricing strategies

There are a number of different pricing strategies that can be used by businesses. A business will use different pricing strategies for different products in its portfolio.

Table 2.10 Advantages and disadvantages of different pricing strategies

Pricing strategy	Advantages	Disadvantages
Cost plus: The business calculates the unit cost of a product and then adds a percentage mark-up for profit, e.g. it costs PC World £300 to purchase a laptop which they then mark up by 50% and sell to the customer for £450.	A quick and easy way of setting the selling price. Ensures that total costs are covered and a profit is generated.	Doesn't cover indirect costs, e.g. other expenses such as rent. Doesn't take external factors into account, e.g. increasing prices during boom periods to maximise profits.
Competitive: The price of a product is set similar to the competitors, e.g. fuel prices.	Avoids a price war. Encourages competition, which improves the market as a whole.	Other elements of the marketing mix must be better than the competition's to ensure sales.
Skimming: The price is set high to begin with and lowers over time, e.g. with electronics, such as the iPad, PS4, etc.	Sufficient 'hype' around a new product enables higher prices to be charged, which can increase profits. Lack of competition also allows maximum prices to be charged.	High initial prices can put off some customers. Technique results in low initial sales numbers.
Penetration: The price is set low to begin with and increases over time, e.g. 'trial prices' on new chocolate bars.	Encourages customers to try a new product. The business hopes to gain repeat custom once the price rises.	Very little profit can be generated during the initial low price period. Could result in a price war if competitors set lower prices too.
Price discrimination: Prices are altered depending on a discriminating factor, e.g. different prices are often charged in the transport industries depending on age, such as a child price, adult price and senior citizen price.	Ensures products appeal to different market segments. Allows for high profit margins on some price brackets.	Harder to budget for sales revenue in advance. Loss in potential revenue from selling at a cheaper price, e.g. a child taking a seat at a football match that could have attracted the full price from an adult.
Destroyer/predatory: The price is deliberately set extremely low for a period of time to force out competitors.	Competitors are forced out of the market, then prices can increase again. Increases market share.	Can only be used by larger companies that can afford to make losses while prices are low. This illegal practice could breach the CMA's anti-competition regulations (see page 24).
Loss leaders: A **promotional** price of one or more products is set unprofitably low to entice customers in to buy other products.	Creates greater footfall, i.e. brings customers to the business. Hopefully, customers will buy normal-priced products while buying loss leaders. Encourages repeat purchases.	There is a risk that some customers will only buy the loss leaders, impacting on profits.

Pricing strategy	Advantages	Disadvantages
Psychological: The price is set just below the next rounded number, e.g. £49.99 instead of £50.	Makes the customer *think* the product is much cheaper than it actually is. Products fit price bands customers have in mind, for example, pricing a car at £9,999.99 instead of the rounded up £10,000 means a customer looking for a 'sub £10,000' car would consider it and it would show up on internet searches with <£10,000 as the search criteria.	Calculating total money owed or giving change can be more difficult. Some customers may ignore the attempt at making the product seem cheaper so the rest of the marketing mix would have to convince them to purchase.

Factors affecting pricing strategy

Table 2.11 contains factors that can affect the pricing strategy chosen.

Table 2.11 Factors affecting the pricing strategy chosen

Factor	Description
Target market for the product	Mass-market products need to be priced in a way that will appeal to most income segments, whereas exclusive products aimed at wealthy segments can be priced higher.
Demand for the product	If the demand for a product is high, then the business can maximise profits by setting the price high; once demand drops, it can lower the price to encourage sales, e.g. the most popular Christmas toy each year is always in high demand, so sells for a high price. 'January sales' are a result of demand dropping after the Christmas rush.
Objectives of the business	If the objective is to maximise sales, a lower price might be offered. If the objective is to maximise profits, a higher price may be set.
External factors	Prices should be lowered during a recession to encourage sales or increased during boom periods to maximise profits. Similarly, prices may have to be lowered to respond to the prices offered by competitors.
Cost of the product	Any pricing strategy should take into account the cost to produce the product (unit cost) as well as other costs that need to be covered, such as rent. For this reason, loss leaders and destroyer pricing should be used sparingly and for short periods.

Activity 2.3

Finding real and current examples of pricing strategies will help you remember them, so you are going to make your own 'prices scrapbook'.

1 Use the internet, newspapers, catalogues or promotional materials to find examples of a product for each pricing strategy.
2 Print or cut out and stick a picture of each product onto a poster, blank booklet or your jotter, or copy and paste images onto a blank document in a word-processing or desktop publishing package on your computer.
3 Describe each pricing strategy beside each product example; be sure to give advantages and disadvantages.
4 Present your findings to others and make sure you keep your finished work to help you revise pricing strategies later.

Quick questions 2.4

1 Describe the cost plus pricing strategy.
2 Identify the pricing strategy that starts low then rises.
3 Suggest two factors that can affect the pricing strategy of a product.
4 Describe what is meant by price discrimination.
5 Outline two advantages of using a 'skimming' strategy.

Topic 14
Marketing mix: place

What you should know

★ Direct selling
★ Using wholesalers
★ Using retailers
★ Factors affecting channels of distribution

Channels of distribution

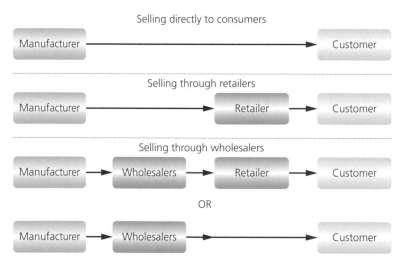

Figure 2.4 Channels of distribution

Channels of distribution are the possible routes taken by a product to reach the consumer from the manufacturer.

Factors affecting the channel of distribution

Table 2.12 shows factors that can affect the channel of distribution that is chosen by a business for a particular product.

Table 2.12 Factors affecting channels of distribution

Factor	Description
Finance available	A manufacturer may not have the finance available to set up e-commerce or print catalogues to sell direct, so using wholesalers or retailers are the only options.
Desired image for the product	Certain products have images that dictate where they can be sold, e.g. Hugo Boss only sell in retailers that have built up a good reputation over at least 5 years.
Shelf life of the product	Some products need to be shipped to retailers fast as they will go out of date quickly, e.g. fresh fruit.
Legal restrictions	Some products can't be sold through certain channels, e.g. prescription medicines need to be sold through pharmacists.
Stage of the product life cycle	Products may only be sold in exclusive outlets at the beginning of a product's life cycle, but may be sold in discount stores during their decline stage to encourage sales.
Technical qualities of the product	Highly technical products may need to be demonstrated, which means personal selling is the ideal channel.

Direct selling

Direct selling means selling direct to the consumer from the manufacturer. This is the shortest channel of distribution and means there are less 'middle men' taking a cut of the profits. Businesses also retain control of *how* their product is marketed.

Table 2.13 contains methods of direct selling that a business could use.

Table 2.13 Advantages and disadvantages of different methods of direct selling

Method	Advantages	Disadvantages
E-commerce: A business sells its products using the internet, e.g. ASOS.	Customers in the global market can be reached 24/7. An entire range can be shown online. Online discounts can be offered to attract customers. Product information and customer comments can sway purchasing decisions.	It can take a lot of time and expense to design attractive, high-quality websites. Customers might be wary of providing their personal details online. Customers need to have access to the internet. Customers need to wait for products to arrive and may have to pay delivery costs.
Mail order: A business sells its products using a catalogue, which is usually sent directly to the customer, e.g. MandM Direct.	Credit facilities are often offered to customers. Customers can browse for products and place orders from home, at a time that suits them. Mail-order-only companies save money on staffing and store costs.	Glossy catalogues can be expensive to produce. Producing catalogues is not environmentally friendly and may not meet CSR aims (see page 11). A level of bad debt might be incurred.

Method	Advantages	Disadvantages
Direct mail: A business posts letters, leaflets and brochures directly to the customer.	Specific market segments can be targeted, e.g. by inserting supermarket recipe cards inside cookery magazines. A wide geographical area can be targeted by placing leaflets inside newspapers and magazines.	Customers can perceive this as 'junk mail' and simply throw it away. Customer mailing lists can quickly become out of date, meaning a business may target the wrong people and waste money.
Personal selling: A salesperson sells products directly to the customer, often by going 'door to door' or over the phone (telesales).	Allows a demonstration or explanation of the product to be given. Feedback on products can be gathered from customers.	Customers can find this type of selling a nuisance and may not be keen to listen. Staffing costs and commission make this method expensive and increasingly unpopular with businesses.
Shopping channels: A business sells products on the TV using dedicated shopping channels, e.g. QVC.	Customers can see products being modelled and demonstrated. Customers can be encouraged to buy on impulse due to short-term bargain prices.	Customers need to switch on to the channel before they can be targeted. Customers need to wait for products to arrive and may have to pay delivery costs.

Retailers

Manufacturers selling products through a **retailer** have the following advantages and disadvantages:

Table 2.14 Advantages and disadvantages of selling through a retailer

Advantages	Disadvantages
Retailers are located close to customers.	Retailers take a cut of the profits.
Retailers often promote the product for the manufacturer.	Retailers may alter the price of the product and so have an effect on the image of the product.
Retailers employ sales assistants to help sell the product.	The product will face competition from other products stocked by the retailer.
Larger retailers buy in bulk.	

Trends in retailer types

The different retailer types have changed in recent years. High street stores, once the standard retail environment, are now much less common. If you think of your local high street you will probably be thinking of bakeries and takeaways, hair salons, barbers, nail bars and, of course, restaurants, pubs and bookmakers. Depending on the size of the town, there may be a few shops trading in other items such as clothing, jewellery and pharmaceuticals. Why just these shops? Well, these remain on the average Scottish high street as these are the businesses that people *have to physically go to*, for example to get a haircut, to eat, etc. Other markets are increasingly catered for online or in one of the other types of retailer, shown in Table 2.15 below.

Figure 2.5 Glasgow Fort retail park has the amenities, choice and infrastructure to entice customers

Table 2.15 Advantages and disadvantages of different types of retailer

Retailer type	Advantages	Disadvantages
Hypermarkets and superstores: There has been a growth in massive supermarkets, which sell many goods and services under one roof. The largest of these are known as hypermarkets, e.g. Tesco Extra.	Most hypermarkets open 24/7. A huge range of products is offered to customers.	Lack of competition from high-street stores can lead to poorer quality products.
Convenience supermarkets: Due to changing work patterns and lifestyle changes, there has been a growth in smaller supermarkets appearing in convenient locations, such as M&S Simply Food or Little Waitrose in city centres, near transport hubs or on forecourts.	Cater for the changing needs of customers so are guaranteed footfall. Prices can be slightly higher than larger supermarkets due to the convenience factor.	Limited choice of products due to smaller store sizes. There can be high levels of waste as it is harder to predict customer numbers than it is for larger, more traditional supermarkets.
Out-of-town retail parks: Out-of-town (OOT) retailing is now found on the outskirts of most major towns in the UK, with good infrastructure such as road links and free car parking, e.g. Glasgow Fort.	Infrastructure attracts customers. Often near amenities such as restaurant chains and cinemas, which can increase footfall. Larger store sizes mean a good product range for low prices due to bulk buying by OOT retailers.	Limited choice of stores compared to high-street shopping or more traditional shopping malls. Only suitable for customers with access to transport. 'Showrooming' can occur, where customers view/try products in store but buy online for a lower price.
Online retailers: Amazon is the biggest online retailer (dubbed 'e-tailer') in the UK. Rather than setting up their own e-commerce site, some manufacturers will sell through retailers like this.	Products can be sold to a worldwide market by online retailers. Products can be sold 24/7.	Customers can't try or touch the product before buying. Delivery charges may put some customers off.
Discount stores: In response to the recession, discount stores have become popular in the UK over the last few years, e.g. B&M Homestores, Home Bargains and the German discount supermarkets, Lidl and Aldi.	Products are sold for rock-bottom prices, which attracts customers looking for value.	Limited product range compared to other retailers. Some customers don't like the image of discount stores.
Department stores: Often flagship stores of any shopping mall or town centre, stores such as John Lewis and Debenhams sell a huge variety of items from clothing to beauty products to home furnishings.	Many target markets can be catered for. Central locations can attract customers, commuters, tourists, etc. Can benefit from impulse buying, e.g. a customer might go to get a perfume but leave with much more as items 'catch their eye'.	More and more department stores are closing due to the high rents and other expenses for the prime retail sites they often occupy. Staff supervision can be difficult.

Case study 2.2
Supermarket wars!

The big four supermarkets in the UK have been adapting the types of retail outlet they offer customers over the past few years. Tesco, the market leader in the UK, has many 'Tesco Superstores' and 'Tesco Extra' branded hypermarkets as well as 'Tesco Metro' and 'Tesco Express' convenience supermarkets. In 2018 Tesco launched a budget store called 'Jack's', named after Tesco founder Jack Cohen.

Figure 2.6 Two of the 'Big 4' supermarkets in the UK – Tesco and Sainsbury's

Sainsbury's, on the other hand, does not have a specific hypermarket brand, but many of its larger stores are the same size as competing Tesco hypermarkets. However, Sainsbury's does offer 'Sainsbury's Local' convenience supermarkets in many towns, cities and transport hubs. In 2018 Sainsbury's announced it was going to merge with Asda – making it the 2nd largest supermarket behind Tesco.

Smaller supermarket chains such as Waitrose and M&S have also recently joined the trend for setting up convenience supermarkets in city centres, train stations and petrol station forecourts, called Little Waitrose and M&S Simply Food respectively. The newest players in the UK supermarket 'war' are, of course, Aldi and Lidl. The German discount stores are doing better than ever with one recent poll concluding that over 60% of households visited either of the stores during a 12-week period.

Discussion points

In pairs, groups or on your own:

1 Suggest reasons for Tesco having such a vast range of stores.
2 Explain why Aldi and Lidl are seeing an increase in customer numbers.
3 Suggest the benefits of having smaller stores such as Sainsbury's Local.
4 Explain why Tesco has launched Jack's.
5 Suggest 4 reasons why Sainsbury's wanted to merge with Asda.

WWW

Visit **https://www.google.com/earth/** to find different types of retailers in your town. Print out images and add them to your notes to aid your revision of this topic.

Wholesalers

Manufacturers can sell goods to **wholesalers** to distribute to smaller retailers or direct to customers. Using a wholesaler has the following advantages and disadvantages for *manufacturers*:

Table 2.16 Advantages and disadvantages for manufacturers of using a wholesaler

Advantages for manufacturers	Disadvantages for manufacturers
Packaging and displaying of goods is carried out by the wholesaler, saving the manufacturer time and costs.	Manufacturers make less profit as a cut is taken by wholesalers.
Wholesalers buy in bulk, saving manufacturers from making lots of smaller deliveries.	The manufacturer loses control of how the product is marketed.

Advantages for manufacturers	Disadvantages for manufacturers
Wholesalers can promote products to retailers, which saves the manufacturer promotion costs.	The manufacturer loses control of which retailers the product is sold to.
The wholesaler carries the risk of products going out of fashion as manufacturers get rid of goods as soon they are produced.	

There are also advantages and disadvantages of using a wholesaler for *retailers*:

Table 2.17 Advantages and disadvantages for retailers of using a wholesaler

Advantages for retailers	Disadvantages for retailers
Retailers can save on storage facilities by buying smaller quantities from wholesalers than they would get from manufacturers.	It is more expensive than going directly to manufacturers as wholesalers add on a margin of profit.
Retailers can benefit from promotions offered by wholesalers that they may not get direct from manufacturers.	Wholesalers offer the same products to retailers' competitors, so other areas of the marketing mix have to be relied on.
Retailers can trial smaller orders of newer products and not be left with large amounts of unsold inventory.	The retailer may miss out on exclusivity deals by not going direct to manufacturers.

Quick questions 2.5

1　Describe two methods of direct selling.
2　Outline three advantages of 'out-of-town' retail parks.
3　Give two reasons for the downturn in department-store custom.
4　Describe an advantage of a manufacturer selling through a retailer.
5　Describe the term 'wholesaler'.

Topic 15
Marketing mix: promotion

What you should know

★ Into-the-pipeline promotions
★ Out-of-the-pipeline promotions
★ Public relations

Promotion is the process of raising awareness of products and persuading customers to buy them.

Into-the-pipeline promotions

Into-the-pipeline sales promotions are offered by the *manufacturer* to encourage *retailers* to purchase products from them.

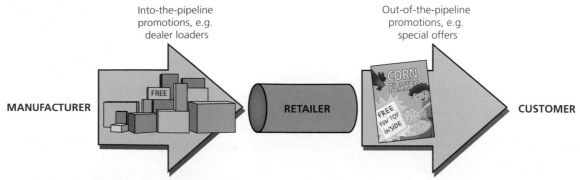

Figure 2.7 Into- and out-of-the-pipeline sales promotions

Figure 2.8 Point of sale materials can help products stand out

Table 2.18 Into-the-pipeline sales promotions methods, with advantages and disadvantages

Method	Advantages	Disadvantages
Trade credit: Manufacturers offer retailers credit to pay for goods at a later date.	No cash is required to stock products, which is good for new or struggling businesses. Retailers can purchase goods and then pay for them once they are sold.	This could lead to bad debt if retailers are unable to sell the goods and repay the supplier.
Point of Sale (POS) materials: Free posters and display materials are given to retailers to display products to customers.	This can enhance the look of the retail store. It can draw customers' eyes to the product display.	Retailers may need to dispose of bulky display materials at the end of the promotion.
Sale or return: Manufacturers give retailers the option to return goods that do not sell.	It allows retailers to try new products without the risk of being stuck with unsold inventory. It improves cashflow.	Products may be returned in a poor condition, creating waste.
Dealer loaders: Discounts used to encourage retailers to stock up on a product, e.g. buy ten boxes get one free.	Retailers can save on the unit cost of products, allowing for greater profits. Savings can be passed to customers to increase sales revenue.	Retailers may overstock and find they are unable to sell. Products might go out of date or out of fashion.
Staff training: Manufacturers can offer retail staff free training to give them the skills and knowledge to sell the product.	Staff become experts in the product, which can impress customers. The quality and motivation of staff are improved.	Training has to be done during normal hours, which reduces productivity, or after hours, which will increase overtime pay.

Out-of-the-pipeline promotions

Out-of-the-pipeline sales promotions are offered by the *retailer* to encourage *customers* to purchase products from them.

Figure 2.9 Loyalty cards can encourage repeat custom

Table 2.19 Out-of-the-pipeline sales promotions methods, with advantages and disadvantages

Method	Advantages	Disadvantages
Special offers: This can include Buy One Get One Free (BOGOF) and other short-term promotions on selected items.	This can encourage customers to try new products, which they may then purchase again at normal price.	Customers might feel pressured into buying more than they need, which may result in waste.
Free gifts: Used to tempt customers to buy a product again or for the first time, e.g. a free toy in children's cereal.	Gifts that require multiple tokens/stamps can encourage repeat purchases.	It can be difficult to find a gift that appeals to all target markets, e.g. a free toy that suits boys and girls.
Vouchers and coupons: Usually given in newspapers/magazines to give customers money off future purchases.	Customers feel they are getting better value for money, which attracts new customers. It can encourage repeat purchases.	Discounts offered by money-off vouchers can reduce profits. Some customers will only spend up to the value of the money-off voucher, limiting sales.
Loyalty schemes: Allow customers to collect points by making purchases, which can then be exchanged for discounts or free products in the future, e.g. Tesco Clubcard.	Information on customer habits and preferences can be gathered. Promotions can be targeted to reflect actual customer preferences.	Customers can be wary if they feel the scheme will be difficult to set up or opt out of. These are time consuming and expensive to implement.
Interest-free credit: Retailers offer customers credit to pay for goods at a later date.	Allows customers to purchase products and then pay for them when they can afford to.	This could lead to bad debt if many customers are unable to pay by the agreed date.
Free trials/sample packs: Services like Netflix and Audible offer a free trial for a month. New products are often given away as a sample, e.g. perfume in a magazine.	Customers can try the product and if they like it, will purchase at full price. Word of mouth can spread from customers enjoying free trials or samples.	Some customers only use the free trial, which will cost the business with no return. It is possible for customers to use a free trial multiple times.
Competitions: Businesses can use competitions to encourage customers to buy in order to take part, for example the popular McDonald's Monopoly.	Can encourage repeat custom as customers try to win or collect more tokens. Can create hype and excitement around a product, which can lead to new custom.	Prizes can cost substantial amounts of money. The associated marketing costs of the competitions can be high and often packaging has to be redesigned.

Method	Advantages	Disadvantages
Trade shows and events: Attending industry trade shows or events such as the Royal Highland Show to give out samples and engage with the public.	Feedback from customers can be gained. Giving out merchandise can spread word/images of the brand.	Some shows have very high rates for a stall. Large quantities of free goods have to be given away for maximum impact

Public relations

Public relations (PR) is the act of controlling the image of a business that is perceived by the public. Some larger businesses have their own dedicated PR Department. Various methods are used by PR to improve the image of an organisation including managing **social media** accounts or launching **apps**, which are both covered in more detail later in this chapter.

Press conferences

The media are invited to a business presentation, where they are given information or news. A new or updated product might be launched.

Table 2.20 Advantages and disadvantages of press conferences

Advantages	Disadvantages
Businesses can send a message or update out to a wide audience while keeping control, to a certain extent, of what is reported.	Could have to face difficult questions and be put on the spot.
It can help to get the media 'on side' and allows the press the opportunity to ask questions to the business directly.	The business could end up making the situation worse in front of the press if they are under-prepared.

Press releases

The media are provided with a written account of a business's newsworthy activities or events. Updated mission statements may also be released to the media.

Table 2.21 Advantages and disadvantages of press releases

Advantages	Disadvantages
This can be used to counteract bad publicity.	Can take a long time to ensure wording is perfect, especially if the business is already under pressure due to a mistake.
Businesses can send out messages or updates without being subject to further questioning.	

Donations to charities

Some businesses donate to charities anonymously, while others will take the opportunity for a good public relations event.

Table 2.22 Advantages and disadvantages of donating to charities

Advantages	Disadvantages
Promotes the CSR aims of the business and can make them seem ethical (see page 11).	Some shareholders may prefer money is invested in growing the business.
This can help the business achieve a positive image.	

Sponsorship

Some businesses pay to sponsor an event, team or venue. This is popular in the sporting industry.

Table 2.23 Advantages and disadvantages of sponsorship

Advantages	Disadvantages
Businesses can benefit from the successes of those that they sponsor.	It can cost a lot to sponsor big events. Virgin Money, for example, paid over £15m to sponsor the London Marathon.
This can help businesses to become popular with customers who visit/support the sponsored event, team or venue.	If an event or team suffers bad PR itself then the business will be associated with it.

Company visits

Businesses may choose to open up their factories to the public for a limited period.

Table 2.24 Advantages and disadvantages of company visits

Advantages	Disadvantages
Customers are able to get a sense of what the business is like and how it is run.	A dedicated staff member or team will have to show visitors around, affecting their productivity elsewhere.

Promotional merchandise

This is giving out free stationery, key rings, even items like golf balls with the company logo and contact information on them.

Table 2.25 Advantages and disadvantages of promotional merchandise

Advantages	Disadvantages
Customers are reminded of the company each time they use the item.	Merchandise can be expensive to provide and has no immediate return.
Everyone likes a free gift! Customers feel rewarded and are more likely to return to the business.	Cheap-looking free gifts can adversely affect the image of the business, even if they are given out for free.
Merchandise such as pens can be passed on to other people which means repeat exposure to the brand name, web address, etc.	

Case study 2.3

Virgin Money London Marathon

Virgin Money has sponsored the London Marathon for over a decade. The London Marathon is a worldwide event and one of the top five marathons in the world with over 30,000 competitors and a TV audience of millions.

Through Virgin Money's charity brand, Virgin Money Giving, runners can collect donations to give to the charity of their choice. This facility is provided free of charge by Virgin Money and the powerful and slick website and app have helped generate record donations by runners and their friends and families.

Figure 2.10 PR in action for Virgin

Virgin's logo is, of course, very visible during the event: on signage, hot air balloons and on every runner's vest. Their brand logo is further promoted on water bottles, hats, lanyards and on the medals, which just about every finisher will post to their social media feeds!

$\Rightarrow$

Discussion points
In pairs, groups or on your own:

1   Explain why Virgin's sponsorship of the London Marathon will make them look good to the public.
2   Discuss all the methods used by Virgin to promote positive PR.
3   Suggest other PR methods Virgin could use associated to this event.

Product endorsement

Product endorsement involves businesses using celebrities (also known as **celebrity endorsement**) to promote the product. For example, Adidas pay Lionel Messi to wear their football boots and appear in their adverts.

Table 2.26 Advantages and disadvantages of product endorsements

Advantages	Disadvantages
The use of a celebrity will make consumers who like the celebrity more likely to purchase the product to be like them.	Some consumers will be put off a product if they don't like the celebrity that has been chosen to endorse it.
The product will be advertised for free every time the celebrity is spotted wearing or using it in public.	If a celebrity gains bad publicity it will tarnish the image of the products they are associated with.
If a celebrity gets good media coverage (e.g. winning a sports event), it will provide positive exposure for the product they are associated with.	It can be very expensive to pay celebrities to endorse products.
Higher prices can be charged as the use of a celebrity gives the product exclusivity.	Poor performance by celebrities (e.g. a sports star losing a sports event or an actor appearing in a box office flop), will result in lower sales of the products they endorse.
Brand loyalty can be created for as long as the celebrity is involved in the endorsement.	

Product placement

Product placement involves businesses paying for products to appear in films, TV shows or video games, for example, the brand of juice characters drink, the clothing brands they wear or the make of car they drive.

Table 2.27 Advantages and disadvantages of product placement

Advantages	Disadvantages
Awareness of products is generated, often to worldwide audiences.	The time of exposure can be very short, limiting the chances of consumers remembering the product they have seen.
It is a form of subliminal advertising – the audience doesn't know they are watching a promotion, they just watch the film.	Often, as a result of bidding wars with rival brands to secure the rights to appear in films, TV shows and games, product placement can cost a lot of money.
Products that can be identified with characters who customers like, can result in sales, as they want to be like the character or the actor who plays them.	Consumers may be put off certain products if they are associated with characters they don't like.
Merchandise 'spin-offs' can be sold, increasing sales on the back of a successful placement, e.g. the Wilson 'Hand' Volleyball from *Castaway*.	Products can appear as part of a negative storyline which can put customers off.

Case study 2.4
Back to the Future

In 1985, the science fiction film *Back to the Future* was the first film to use product placement on a large scale. The Irish sports car DeLorean featured prominently as the 'time machine' in the movie. Many other brands appear in it, such as Pepsi, Kellogg's, Pizza Hut and Toyota, either as main props used by characters or just appearing in the background. The main character, Marty McFly, even wore futuristic 'power laces' Nike trainers in the fictional future year of 2015, which Nike have now produced for real!

Figure 2.11 Product placement

If you ever watch the film (or the entire trilogy!) be sure to watch out for the product placement.

Discussion points
In pairs, groups or on your own:

1   Explain why products being used by characters in TV and film is a good method of promotion.
2   Suggest the advantages of using products in a film about time travel.
3   Explain reasons why Nike produced the fictional trainers for real, in 2015.
4   Suggest other well-known products used in films you have seen.

Factors affecting methods of promotion

The following factors can affect the promotion method chosen.

- **The target market** – Businesses should promote their products in places where they are likely to be seen by the target market. Market research feedback will help with this.
- **The finance available** – Every business would love to advertise at half time during the World Cup final but only the biggest marketing budgets will stretch to this.
- **The marketing mix** – All elements of the marketing mix should work in **synergy**. This means the methods are more effective when combined even though they work well as stand-alone elements. For example, the promotion of a model of GHD hair straighteners near the end of their life cycle (product) should be advertised in fashion magazines (promotion) informing the target market of a reduction in price if they buy them online (place).
- **Ethical practices** – Promotions should be **ethical** in order to avoid upsetting others. For example, promotions should not:
  - mislead customers
  - be indecent
  - make false claims designed to harm the competition.

Quick questions 2.6

1   Outline two into-the-pipeline promotions.
2   Justify the use of free trials as a promotional activity.
3   Describe three methods a PR department could use to improve a business's image.
4   Outline one disadvantage and one advantage of giving a press conference.
5   Define the following PR activities:
    a) Celebrity endorsement
    b) Product placement

Topic 16
Extended marketing mix

The final three 'P's
People

These final three 'P's are geared towards the marketing of the service customers receive. This is especially important for businesses operating in the tertiary sector, such as hotels, restaurants and banks; however, all businesses will have to provide services to customers at some point.

People refers to *who* is representing a business or a brand. Those employed by the business are essential to the image and reputation of a business, especially those that are **customer facing**, such as customer service assistants, receptionists and sales staff. The following steps should ensure the 'people' element of the marketing mix is successful:

Table 2.28 The 'people' element of the marketing mix

Method	Justification
Train staff well to deal with customers effectively.	This enables staff to be informed of the expectations of the business when dealing with customers, such as being polite and helpful.
Regularly update staff on product/service developments.	This ensures staff appear knowledgeable and can assist customers.
Ensure selection methods (see Topic 21) are rigorous and staff aren't appointed on a 'whim'.	This ensures the people employed are suitable to represent the business and its values.
Monitor staff, e.g. by recording customer-service calls or sending mystery shoppers.	This ensures employees are representing the business appropriately and standards are maintained.
Provide an effective after-sales service. This includes having helpful and friendly staff who make sure the customer stays satisfied with their purchase.	Effective after-sales can ensure the customer returns to the business, for example to get a car serviced. A good experience during the life of the product will also ensure the business is the first port of call when it comes to buying a new product.

Remember

The 'people' in a business are so important to ensuring repeat custom. Think of a time you experienced rude or ineffective **customer service**. That is what businesses need to avoid!

Process

Process refers to *how* a customer receives a service. This could be the *process* they go through to book a holiday, obtain a bank loan or even just select and pay for goods in a shop. The following steps should ensure the 'process' element of the marketing mix is successful:

Table 2.29 The 'process' element of the marketing mix

Method	Justification
Ensure that outlets and call centres are well staffed.	This avoids customers having to queue for too long, which can put them off returning.
Offer 'live chat' or 'FAQ' services on the business's website.	This reduces the number of customers making queries either on the phone or in person.
Empower customer-facing staff to make decisions.	This avoids further waiting as problems or queries do not need to be passed on to management.
Regularly assess processes such as queues or ordering times.	This helps the business understand where problems lie and allows them to be addressed. Serpentine (zig zag) queues can be introduced to speed up waiting times.
Introduce the latest technologies to improve processes.	Technology is generally faster than humans and will speed up processes, e.g. self-checkouts in supermarkets and touchscreen ordering in McDonald's.

Physical evidence

Physical evidence refers to *what* customers see that gives them clues about a business from the image it portrays. The following steps should ensure the 'physical evidence' element of the marketing mix is successful:

Table 2.30 The 'physical evidence' element of the marketing mix

Method	Justification
Premises and vehicles should be modern and clean.	This ensures that customers' opinion of the business isn't ruined by old-fashioned or dirty shops, reception areas or delivery vans.
Settings should convey the type of ambiance to match the product or service on offer.	This ensures that customers feel that their needs are recognised even before they purchase a good or service, e.g. the stylish and relaxing setting of an upmarket hair salon compared to the fun and colourful setting of a theme park.
Feedback and testimonials from previous customers should be promoted.	This provides reference materials for new customers which is especially important when purchasing a service as it can't be tried beforehand.
The layout and design of websites should be carefully considered.	The website should convey to the customer the type of business it is. Careful consideration should be given to colour schemes, fonts and images. If they reflect the business well the website will appeal to the target market.

Remember

The 'extended P's' of the marketing mix are mostly concerned with tertiary (service) sector businesses.

Case study 2.5

Nando's

Everyone loves a 'cheeky Nando's'! The Afro-Portuguese 'fast-casual' restaurant offering peri-peri chicken dishes is a UK favourite.

Uniquely designed (no outlet is the same), featuring spirited Afro-Portuguese music, pictures, statues and a self-collect cutlery and condiment station, Nando's has sought to set itself apart from other fast-dining restaurants. Staff enjoy the relaxed atmosphere and are given plenty of training and benefits, which all help to make them and therefore their customers smile! Nando's has managed to cater for and market themselves successfully to different social demographics that wouldn't usually frequent the same places. Families having a day off from home-cooked dinners; excitable groups of teenagers looking to grab a bite before a wild night – even the British royalty get their takeaways from Nando's.

Figure 2.12 A typical Nando's restaurant

They have even managed to do all this without a single TV or radio advert. It is all about the Nando's PR machine, including celebrity 'tweets' from the likes of Ed Sheeran and David Beckham. Even the phrase 'cheeky Nando's' injects the brand into everyday conversation and apparently there is a 'secret menu' that will get people talking – and tweeting – about the company.

Discussion points

In pairs, groups or on your own:

1   Give examples of Nando's physical evidence element of the marketing mix.
2   Give examples of Nando's process element of the marketing mix.
3   Give examples of Nando's people element of the marketing mix.
4   Explain the advantages of Nando's PR activities.

 Activity 2.4

- Find out about the extended marketing mix of a business of your choice.
- Prepare a presentation or poster and try to include information with supporting images for **ALL 7 Ps**.

This will be good practice for your assignment if you are interested in this topic area!

Quick questions 2.7

1   Suggest three ways in which a business can ensure the 'people' element of the marketing mix is effective.
2   Outline two ways in which technology can speed up the process of serving customers.
3   Describe ways in which a website can convey the desired image of a business.

Key questions 2.2 (?)

1 **Explain** how two elements of the marketing mix can be improved to enhance the effectiveness of a large organisation.
2 **Describe** two advantages and two disadvantages of having a varied product portfolio.

Use of technology in marketing

Evidence of the use of technology in marketing has been abundant throughout this chapter. However, here is a summary of how technology can be used in the marketing function.

- The internet can be used to obtain market information from surveys or competitors' websites.
- The internet can also be used to advertise products, targeted through browsing histories.
- E-commerce can be used to sell products online.
- Social media can be used to interact with customers.
- Databases can be used to keep customer records and can be easily searched and merged into direct mail shots.
- Apps can be used to engage with customers, promote or sell products.
- SMS texts can be sent alerting customers of promotions.
- EPOS can be used to gain market research information.
- Self-checkout systems can be used to speed up the process of purchasing products.
- Digital screens can be used to display eye-catching advertisements.
- 3D can be used in cinemas and on TV to capture customers' attention during advertisements.

Social media

Social media sites such as Facebook and Twitter are being used increasingly by businesses to communicate with customers. Businesses also use social media accounts as a PR tool by responding to comments from customers.

Table 2.31 Advantages and disadvantages of social media as a promotion method

Advantages	Disadvantages
The target market can be contacted directly, as they have 'liked' or 'followed' the business's social media page. This saves marketing to uninterested consumers.	It can be difficult to engage with new customers as they have to voluntarily agree to see the business's updates.
Information on new products or promotional offers, price changes or new products can be uploaded immediately.	It requires a lot of time to use social media effectively; larger businesses will have to employ someone to engage with social media full time.
The business can analyse those that like or follow them to find out their location/age/gender, which can allow them to target others effectively.	Negative feedback can be given, which can put other customers off using the business.
Consumers can leave comments which can be used to improve the product.	Negative feedback can be given instantly, not allowing the business time to release a statement in its defence.
Social media is free to use.	

Apps

Many businesses are now using **apps** designed for tablet computers and smartphones to promote their business. For example, Apple recently bought Beats in a $3 billion **takeover** (see page 18) primarily to acquire their *Music* app.

Table 2.32 Advantages and disadvantages of using apps for promotional purposes

Advantages	Disadvantages
Can target 'in-app' promotions and information on products that users will like, based on their browsing history.	Apps require a mobile signal to be used, limiting the reach to customers in rural locations.
Users of apps can share their experiences on social media sites, allowing the business free promotion and wider recognition.	There is a limit to the amount of information that can be put on apps due to the screen size of mobile devices.
Apps can have integrated services, such as airlines' online check-in services or online banking apps which increase usability.	Apps cost money to develop and are often given away for free.
E-commerce (known as m-commerce on mobile devices) can be integrated, increasing sales potential to worldwide, 24/7.	Most apps, especially 'fun' apps that aim to promote businesses in a subliminal way, e.g. Nike's World Cup game app, have a very short shelf-life.
Information about products and offers can be updated quickly, keeping customers informed thus giving the organisation a good channel of communication.	Some customers are very uncertain about making purchases using m-commerce due to less secure virus protection than computers.
The app can integrate games, videos and photographs to grab users' attention and promote the business in a fun and engaging way.	

Quick questions 2.8

1 Suggest three ways in which technology can be used to engage with customers.
2 Describe two benefits of using digital screens rather than traditional billboards to advertise products.
3 Suggest three ways in which smartphones can be used in marketing activities.

Key question 2.3

Describe how two types of technology are used in the marketing function.

Exam-style questions practice – Chapter 2

1 Explain the advantages and disadvantages of desk research. **(4 marks)**

2 Compare the following:

a) Market led and product led

b) Quota sampling and random sampling. **(4 marks)**

3 Explain the effect on profits and sales during the following stages of the product life cycle:

○ Development

○ Growth

○ Saturation. **(6 marks)**

4 Describe activities that would be carried out in the development (R & D) stage of launching a new product. **(5 marks)**

5 Explain the benefits of using a psychological pricing strategy. **(2 marks)**

6 Describe the trends in retailer types in recent years. **(3 marks)**

7 Discuss the advantages and disadvantages of a retailer using a wholesaler rather than going to the manufacturer. **(4 marks)**

8 Discuss the use of social media and mobile apps for interacting with customers. **(6 marks)**

9 Explain ways in which the following extended marketing mix elements can improve customer experience:

a) Physical evidence

b) Process. **(4 marks)**

10 Explain the benefits to a business of using e-commerce. **(4 marks)**

Chapter 3 Management of operations

Inventory management.

What you should know

★ Inventory management control system
★ Just-in-time inventory control
★ Inventory storage and warehousing
★ Logistics

It is the role of the operations department to provide the products that the organisation offers. Secondary sector organisations will be concerned with actually producing goods from raw materials, whereas tertiary sector will be concerned with the purchasing and stocking of goods or the systems that are in place to provide services to customers.

Inventory management is concerned with the sourcing and storage of raw materials (for secondary sector businesses) or supplies of finished goods for resale (for tertiary sector businesses).

Logistical management of inventory

Logistical management of inventory refers to the process of dealing with an entire order from start to finish. Logistics managers will be responsible for the following process:

1 **Inventory** – Liaising with suppliers that provide materials for production, partly or completely finished goods (known as the supply chain).
2 **Storage & warehousing** – Ensuring the appropriate storage of inventory including sending inventory to production departments if required.
3 **Order processing** – Dealing with orders from customers to ensure they receive the correct products.

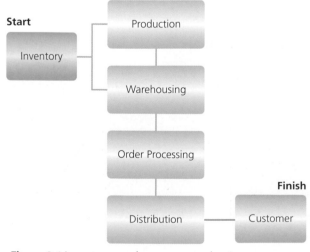

Figure 3.1 Inventory can be sent to production or warehousing ready to be processed

4 **Distribution** – Deciding on the best method of distribution to get the product to the customer. Distribution methods can include:

- Road/rail/air/sea etc.
- Utilities infrastructure
- Satellite/cable/mobile networks

Logistics managers must also be aware of external factors that can affect methods of distribution such as rising fuel costs and environmental pressures such as attempting to reduce their carbon footprint by being more fuel-efficient.

Overstocking and understocking

Once a supplier is chosen, the business must then consider the quantity of inventory to be ordered. A business must not overstock or understock as both have negative consequences.

Table 3.1 The consequences of overstocking and understocking

Consequences of overstocking	Consequences of understocking
Supplies could go out of date if they are stored for too long.	The business may run out of inventory and be unable to continue production or carry on selling.
Supplies could go out of fashion before they are used.	The business will not benefit from bulk buying discounts due to making smaller orders.
Too many supplies leaves a risk of theft by staff, customers or thieves.	There may be no goods to sell, resulting in a bad reputation and customers not returning.
The business will have to pay for stockholding costs, such as insurance and security.	There will be an increase in delivery costs since many smaller deliveries will have to be made.
The **opportunity cost** of money being tied up in inventory which could be better used elsewhere in the business.	There will be an increase in administration costs, e.g. paying staff to browse for supplies, complete order forms, settle invoices, etc.

Hints & tips ★

Although the consequences of over- and understocking are assessed at N5 level they can be used to answer questions across many topics in this chapter.

Inventory management control system

Figure 3.2 illustrates the features of an inventory management system.

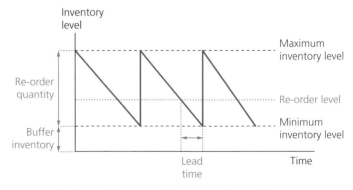

Figure 3.2 Features of an inventory management system

Hints & tips ★

You should be able to draw and label an inventory management diagram accurately.

As you can see from the diagram, the diagonal line illustrates inventory being used over time until it reaches the minimum level. Before the minimum level is reached a re-order level is triggered, allowing inventory to be ordered once the minimum is reached. The vertical line illustrates the inventory level reaching the maximum again. Table 3.2 describes the features in more detail.

Table 3.2 Features of an inventory management system

Feature	Description	Justification
Maximum/ economic inventory level	This is the most amount of inventory that should be held.	Setting this level avoids consequences of overstocking.
Minimum inventory level	This is the least amount of inventory that should be held.	Setting this level avoids consequences of understocking.
Re-order level	The level at which inventory is re-ordered. Computerised inventory systems link to EPOS and automatically re-order goods.	This avoids running out of inventory.
Re-order quantity	This is the amount that is ordered.	This ensures the quantity ordered is not too much or too little.
Lead time	This is the time taken between an order being placed and inventory arriving.	As short a lead time as possible allows the business to react to rush orders.
Buffer inventory	This is the extra inventory below the agreed minimum to be used in emergencies.	This ensures that production doesn't stop and sales continue to be made.

Setting inventory levels

The inventory management system is a guide. Each business will have to set their own specific levels, depending on the following factors:

- The **maximum inventory level** depends on the storage available, the cost of storing goods and the maximum amount of demand.
- The **minimum inventory level** depends on the relationship with suppliers, the skill levels of staff so materials are not wasted, the finance available, the minimum amount of demand and the likelihood of drastic changes to tastes and fashions.
- The **re-order level** depends on lead time, the amount of inventory already held, if bulk-buying discounts are available, and the maximum and minimum inventory levels themselves (see above).

Just-in-time

Just-in-time (JIT) is an alternative approach to inventory management. JIT is the process of ordering supplies only when they are either required for production or when an order is placed by a customer. JIT originated in Japan, a country renowned for 'lean' production techniques that increase efficiency and reduce wastage.

Table 3.3 Advantages and disadvantages of JIT

Advantages	Disadvantages
Allows production to be lean, i.e. there is no wastage as all inventory is used for production.	If deliveries are late then the business will face the negative consequences of understocking.
No money is tied up in inventory, improving cash flow and working capital.	Requires excellent relationships with suppliers to work effectively, which can take time to develop.
No warehouse is required, saving costs.	Relies on a good infrastructure between the business and suppliers, e.g. roads.
The business is more responsive to changing external factors.	No room for error in production.

> **Hints & tips**
>
> The advantages and disadvantages of JIT are similar to those of understocking!

Storage and warehousing

A business has to decide how to store its inventory. Inventory is usually stored in **warehouses**. Large buildings in central locations are used to store inventory and distribute raw materials to factories or finished goods to retail outlets (called **centralised storage**). Warehouses can also be smaller buildings or areas of a factory or retail outlet (called **decentralised storage**).

Centralised storage

This involves storing inventory in one central location in a large, purpose-built **warehouse**.

Centralised storage has the following advantages and disadvantages.

> **Remember**
>
> These are the features of effective warehousing:
> - Ground level only
> - Mechanical handling, e.g. forklifts
> - Suitable environment for products e.g. refrigerated
> - Large loading bay with easy access
> - Technology utilised to improve speed and accuracy, e.g. barcode scanning, robotics

Table 3.4 Advantages and disadvantages of centralised storage

Advantages	Disadvantages
Specialist staff are employed to maintain inventory, which improves speed of inventory handling and security.	Inventory has to be delivered to each division or department, causing delays.
Centralised warehouses can store a massive amount of inventory, benefiting from economies of scale.	Specialist staff need to be employed to maintain inventory, increasing wage costs.
The same procedures for issuing inventory are used across the organisation, improving consistency.	Specialist equipment needs to be purchased and maintained.
It may be cheaper to store inventory in one large warehouse than the total cost of many smaller on-site storerooms.	Inventory usage levels and needs are unclear as divisions need to communicate with the warehouse.
Easier for suppliers to deliver inventory as centralised warehouses are often located close to infrastructure, e.g. motorway networks, docks or air and rail cargo terminals.	The use of centralised warehousing has declined due to more efficient inventory systems such as JIT, sourcing direct from the supplier.

Decentralised storage

This involves storing inventory in many locations in smaller warehouses or store rooms.

Decentralised storage has the following advantages and disadvantages.

Table 3.5 Advantages and disadvantages of decentralised storage

Advantages	Disadvantages
Inventory is always close at hand when needed for production or to sell to customers.	Can lead to wastage or theft of inventory as security isn't as good as it is in centralised storage.
Smaller, more local warehouses are more responsive to local needs.	Lack of specialist staff can lead to inventory control being clumsy and inefficient.
Inventory usage reflects production as it is stored in factories or retail outlets.	Each division may handle inventory differently, leading to inconsistency and problems being harder to pinpoint for senior management.
Smaller amounts of inventory result in no negative consequences of overstocking.	Smaller amounts of inventory result in negative consequences of understocking.

Computerised inventory control

Most inventory systems are now computerised. The advantages of this outweigh the disadvantages as seen in Table 3.6.

Table 3.6 Advantages and disadvantages of computerised inventory control

Advantages	Disadvantages
Databases keep balances of inventory which are automatically updated.	Computerised systems will cost a lot of money to install and maintain.
Can be linked to tills through EPOS, which update inventory levels with each sale.	Money and time need to be invested to train staff to operate the system efficiently.
Accurate and constant monitoring of inventory levels allows for automatic re-ordering.	Crashes and breakdowns can hold up re-orders and production.
Allows for decisions on slow-moving inventory or best sellers to be made by managers from their computers.	
Can highlight regional variations in inventory for head office.	
Can highlight seasonal shifts in demand.	
Is a deterrent to theft by staff as they know inventory levels are monitored closely.	

Case study 3.1

Amazon

Internet e-tailer Amazon couldn't possibly have a store of inventory in every town. Its approach is to have massive centralised warehouses that cater for entire sections of the country. The biggest warehouse in the UK is located near Dunfermline in Fife. It is the size of 14 football pitches! The site is located next to the M90 and A92, so it is within easy reach of Edinburgh, Stirling and St Andrews, as well as towns and cities to the north, south and west.

$\Rightarrow$

Warehouse staff receive, pack and ship items for Amazon customers every day. A central computer records the location of goods and maps out routes for warehouse staff. Staff carry hand-held computer devices which communicate with the central computer and monitor their rate of progress.

Discussion points

In pairs, groups or on your own:

1 Suggest reasons why Amazon's Fife warehouse is a good example of centralised storage.
2 Describe the advantages of the location of Amazon's Fife warehouse.
3 Explain the use of technology at Amazon's Fife warehouse.

The role of the logistics manager

Let's look again at the role of a manager (see page 50) to understand exactly what logistics managers do:

1 *Planning* inventory required using **production** and **sales budgets**
2 *Organising* for the resources needed for logistics, including **warehouse** equipment and staff
3 *Commanding* warehouse staff to carry out tasks
4 *Co-ordinating* the supply chain, channels and methods of distribution so deliveries are made on time
5 *Controlling* the quality, quantity, cost and efficiency of the movement and storage of inventory, etc.
6 *Delegating* inventory procedures to **decentralised** warehouses
7 *Motivating* other members of their team.

Figure 3.3 Logistics is now utilising low emissions trucks to be environmentally friendly and to lower fuel costs

Hints & tips

Don't get confused between channels of distribution and methods of (physical) distribution!

Quick questions 3.1

1 Justify the need for a re-order level.
2 Define just-in-time (JIT) inventory control.
3 Describe two advantages of computerised inventory control.
4 Identify three aspects of logistical management of inventory.
5 Draw and label an inventory control management system.
6 Outline three features of effective warehousing.

Key questions 3.1

1 **Describe** two features of an inventory control management system.
2 **Explain** two purposes of an inventory control management system.

Topic 18
Methods of production

What you should know

★ Capital-intensive, mechanised and automated production
★ Labour-intensive production
★ Factors affecting method of production

Budgeting

Budgeting is not just used by the finance department. In fact, it is also used in operations and marketing.

Sales budgets

Sales budgets are firstly produced by the marketing department. Their purpose is to:
● provide targets for sales staff to aim for
● be used in conjunction with bonuses or commission for meeting targets
● motivate sales staff to reach targets.

Production budgets

Production budgets are created by using information from the sales budget. Their purpose is to:
● plan production so that there are enough goods to meet anticipated sales
● allow enough raw materials to be purchased so there is no understocking
● allow for not too many raw materials to be purchased so there is no overstocking.

Methods of production

Capital-intensive production

Capital-intensive production involves producing products primarily by means of machinery and equipment.

Capital-intensive production can utilise either **automation** or **mechanisation**.

Automation

Automation refers to production being fully *automatic*. This involves the use of **computer aided manufacture** (CAM) to control fully automated assembly lines that use **robotics** as seen in Figure 3.4. Compare this to the picture of the Model T Ford **labour-intensive** production line shown in Figure 3.6.

Figure 3.4 Fully automated, capital-intensive production, using robotics to manufacture cars

Using automation has the following advantages and disadvantages:

Table 3.7 Advantages and disadvantages of automation

Advantages	Disadvantages
CAM/robotics produce products in exactly the same way every time, improving consistency.	Huge investment is needed to automate a production line.
CAM doesn't lose concentration so fewer mistakes are made, which limits waste.	Breakdowns can be catastrophic, losing hours of production time and wasting vast amounts of materials.
Robots can do jobs that are dangerous for humans to do.	Replacing labour with automated robotics will demotivate retained employees.
Robots don't take breaks, holidays or sick leave so can work 24/7.	Absence of a 'human touch', often leads to lack of creativity and personality in the products produced.
Fewer employees are needed as automation doesn't require human control, reducing wage costs.	

Mechanisation

Mechanisation refers to labour and machines working together to produce products. A traditional example is a machinist operating a sewing machine in a textile factory.

Table 3.8 Advantages and disadvantages of mechanisation

Advantages	Disadvantages
Using machinery improves accuracy over purely handmade products as human error is lessened.	The machines and equipment can't be used without humans, so are liable to some human error.
Using machinery can speed up production.	Production can't be 24/7 as humans require breaks, holidays, and so on.
Unlike automation, a human element exists in mechanisation, improving creativity.	If machinery breaks down the business has to repair it, leaving workers idle.

Labour-intensive production

Labour-intensive production involves humans doing *most* of the work. This is most common in **job production**, for example, skilled hand-crafts, such as cake decorating.

Labour-intensive production has the following advantages and disadvantages.

Figure 3.5 Sometimes nimble fingers are best for intricate jobs!

> ### Hints & tips
> Some **mechanisation** could be classed as labour intensive, depending on whether it is the machine or the human doing most of the work, for example, a joiner using power tools.

Table 3.9 Advantages and disadvantages of labour-intensive production

Advantages	Disadvantages
Labour can be less expensive than capital-intensive production.	The business is at high risk of human error, resulting in waste, faulty products and disgruntled customers.
Humans can use initiative and creativity, something that is often lacking in automated systems.	Humans have to take breaks, holidays, etc., which limits production time.
There's a constant supply of labour, often skilled labour, available in areas of the country with manufacturing traditions.	Humans have to be paid overtime for working over normal hours whereas machines cost the same at any time of day.
Employees are motivated as they are not 'giving up' tasks to machines.	Recruitment, training and wage costs need to be considered.

Case study 3.2
Ford

When cars were first invented they were made to order; however, very few cars were sold as they were so expensive. Henry Ford pioneered not only the first *car* assembly line, but the first assembly line to be used to make *any* consumer good in large quantities, known as **mass production**!

The 'Model T' Ford car was the first car to be mass produced. Each car would start off at one end of the assembly line as a basic frame and parts would be added, such as the wheels, engine and bodywork, as it passed

Figure 3.6 The Model T assembly line

on from one section to the next. Unlike modern assembly lines which are mostly **automated** (capital intensive), in 1908 most of the work was done by hand (labour intensive). Each worker would do the same job over and over again. This enabled him to become skilled and fast at doing the job; this is known as **specialisation**. There was one main drawback of the Model T, as Henry Ford said himself, 'You can have it in any colour you want, as long as it's black!'

Discussion points
In pairs, groups or on your own:

1 Suggest reasons why car production was so expensive before the Model T was invented.
2 Explain why assembly lines lower unit costs.
3 Discuss the differences between capital and labour intensive.
4 Explain what you think Henry Ford meant by his famous quote.

Reasons for production choices

The method of production chosen will depend on the following factors.

Table 3.10 Reasons for choosing a production method

Factor	Description
Quantity of goods required	If large quantities are required, capital-intensive production will be more suitable than labour-intensive.
Skills of the workforce	If the workforce is highly skilled, their expertise would be better suited to labour-intensive production.
Cost of labour	Rising labour costs (perhaps due to a rising minimum wage) could mean that the business should move to capital-intensive production.
Finance available	Large amounts of finance are required to equip factories or hire the number of staff needed for large-scale capital-intensive production.
Technology available	If the business doesn't have the technology required for capital-intensive production, labour-intensive is the only option.

Quick questions 3.2

1 Describe two advantages of using automated, capital-intensive production.
2 Discuss one advantage and one disadvantage of labour-intensive production.
3 Describe the meaning of the term 'specialisation'.

Key questions 3.2

1 **Describe** two production methods used by large organisations.
2 **Explain** one advantage and one disadvantage of the methods you described in key question 1 above.

Quality

Importance of quality

It is important for the operations department to ensure goods are of good **quality** for the following reasons:

- Poor-quality goods can result in customers returning their purchases, causing a loss in sales.
- Extremely low quality can result in products not meeting safety standards, which can lead to bad PR.
- Conversely, high-quality goods can result in a good reputation.
- Being associated with quality production can attract high-quality staff.
- The highest-quality goods can be sold for premium prices.

Methods of ensuring quality

Quality control

Quality control is the most basic method of ensuring quality. Quality control is a method of **inspecting** raw materials or finished goods to check they are of an acceptable standard and quality.

Table 3.11 Advantages and disadvantages of quality control

Advantages	Disadvantages
Ensures that faulty goods are not sent to customers.	Can create a lot of waste as the quality of the goods are not checked until they are made and have to be thrown away if they do not meet quality standards.
Limits the potential for a bad reputation due to faulty products.	Products have to be reworked from scratch, costing the business time and money.

Quality assurance

Quality assurance is a method of **prevention**, i.e. where products are checked to see that they are of high quality at different stages in the development and production process rather than just at the end. For example, a **quality assurance manager** might check the raw materials, inspect the machinery, speak to employees, sample work in progress and inspect finished goods.

Table 3.12 Advantages and disadvantages of quality assurance

Advantages	Disadvantages
Less wastage, which decreases costs spent on discarded materials.	Can slow down production as many processes are inspected.
Easy to identify where faults in the production process lie.	Can increase the costs of production, e.g. paying QA managers' wages.

Continual improvement

Organisations should always attempt to improve quality, even if it has met its objectives. This is known as **continual improvement**. A Japanese philosophy known as **kaizen** should be considered by businesses looking to improve. Kaizen is the philosophy of everyone and every process and system in the organisation *continuously improving*.

Table 3.13 Advantages and disadvantages of continual improvement

Advantages	Disadvantages
The business stays ahead of the competition.	The business can have high staff-development costs.
The business can react easily to changing external factors.	Employees may feel under pressure to continually keep improving.

Quality circles

A **quality circle** is another Japanese philosophy on how to improve quality and ensure efficiency. It involves a group of employees meeting with a line manager to discuss problems in the production process and how to solve them. Suggestions are then passed to management for further discussion and may then be implemented.

Table 3.14 Advantages and disadvantages of quality circles

Advantages	Disadvantages
Employees will be motivated as they get to have a say in decision-making.	Employees meet during paid company time, meaning production time is lost.
Management get well-informed suggestions from the workers who actually produce the product.	Employees are often trained to join a quality circle, costing the business even more time and money.

Quality standards and symbols

A **quality standard** or **symbol** proves that a product has met an agreed industry standard, for example, hotels that meet standards to achieve a 'star' rating, such as a 5-star hotel. BSI, the business 'standards company' is renowned for its marks of excellence including the globally recognised BSI Kitemark™. Similarly, products that are deemed safe are awarded the **CE** mark.

Table 3.15 Advantages and disadvantages of quality standards and symbols

Advantages	Disadvantages
Awards prove to customers that a product has met an agreed standard of quality.	Time-consuming processes need to be completed to achieve the award.
Symbols can be used as a promotional tool to gain a competitive edge.	Agreed standards need to be maintained at all times.
Customers will have confidence in purchasing the product and may repeat purchase.	If any award is removed it would give the organisation a poor reputation.
Higher prices can be charged as the product is of high quality.	Annual checks and audits by awarding bodies can disrupt production.

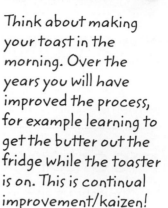

Remember

Think about making your toast in the morning. Over the years you will have improved the process, for example learning to get the butter out the fridge while the toaster is on. This is continual improvement/kaizen!

WWW

Find out more about the BSI by logging on to: **www.bsigroup.com**

Find out more about CE marking by logging on to: **www.gov.uk/ government/ publications** and searching for ce-marking

Case study 3.3
BSI Kitemark

Having a BSI Kitemark associated with a product or service confirms that it has been independently checked to prove that it conforms to a particular standard, and that it has also been checked consistently over time. It is one of the most recognised symbols of quality and safety and offers true value to consumers, businesses and procurement practices.

Figure 3.7 The BSI Kitemark is a sign of quality, safety and trust, reassuring customers that safety standards have been met

The BSI Kitemark originated as the British Standards Mark in 1903 for use on tramway rails when standardisation reduced the number of rail sizes from 75 to 5. The BSI Kitemark can be seen on hundreds of products from manhole covers and security locks to fire extinguishers and riding helmets and includes service related schemes too such as the installation of windows and doors and the repair of vehicles after they have been in an accident. Today the newest BSI Kitemark schemes help consumers identify banking apps they can trust and help banking customers quickly and easily identify financial products they can trust to meet their essential needs.

Discussion points

In pairs, groups or on your own, consider:

Why is it important for:

1 businesses
2 consumers
3 procurement (buying) departments

for products to be awarded the BSI Kitemark?

Quality management

Quality management is a *holistic* approach to ensuring quality products. This means it incorporates not just one method but takes into account a variety of methods, including quality assurance, quality improvement and quality circles. Quality management ensures *all people* in an organisation are committed to quality to ensure **zero errors** occur. Organisations that prove they carry out quality management can be awarded the ISO 9001 quality standard.

> *Hints & tips* ⭐
>
> *'Quality management' brings together many of the quality methods discussed in this chapter.*

Table 3.16 Advantages and disadvantages of quality management

Advantages	Disadvantages
Quality management should result in zero errors, which drastically reduces waste.	Substantial staff training, to ensure no mistakes are made, will increase costs and result in lost work time.
Staff are motivated, as they are constantly consulted on improving quality.	Requires the commitment of *all* staff, which could require a stricter selection process.
Products will be renowned for being of the highest quality, increasing customer confidence and market share.	Processes need to be continually monitored and compared to policies and procedures, which can be time consuming.
A culture of teamwork is established, as everyone works together to improve.	

Mystery shoppers

People are employed, often through an agency, to purchase products, ask questions, register complaints or behave in a certain way, and then provide feedback to the business about the experiences they had.

Figure 3.8 Mystery shopping can ensure a quality service

Table 3.17 Advantages and disadvantages of mystery shopping

Advantages	Disadvantages
The mystery shopper is not employed by or directly connected to the business. This means no bias is shown.	Staff may resent a mystery shopper evaluating them, if they are aware of it, and may take the feedback personally.
Valuable feedback, which may be lost when a customer chooses simply not to buy a product, is gathered when a product is below standard or unsatisfactory.	The mystery shopper's feedback may not be fully representative of the business as a whole as it provides a limited evaluation, i.e. one day, one branch, one customer service assistant, etc.
The mystery shopper can suggest improvements that ensure a better match between the experience that the customer *actually* has and the one the business *intends* them to have.	Allowances have to be made for human error in judgements. Mystery shoppers are people who have feelings and opinions, which may cloud their judgement from time to time.
Dissatisfied customers are likely to share their poor experiences with others, whereas the mystery shopper is *not permitted* to do this.	Businesses need to pay mystery shoppers, often through an agency, increasing costs.

Benchmarking

Benchmarking involves copying the quality of a finished product, and the processes used to achieve it, used by the market leader.

Table 3.18 Advantages and disadvantages of benchmarking

Advantages	Disadvantages
If successful, the product will be as good as the best on the market.	Can be difficult to gain information about other organisation's quality methods.
Saves the business time developing their own approach to ensuring quality.	The business will only ever be 'as good' as the benchmark at a time. The benchmark may improve, leaving the organisation behind. The business will never be better than the benchmark, so will never be market leader.

Quick questions 3.3 ?

1 Suggest two reasons why organisations should ensure quality.
2 Describe two features of quality management.
3 Describe the term 'benchmarking'.
4 Describe two advantages of using mystery shoppers as a method to ensure quality.
5 Suggest three quality standards or symbols an organisation could be awarded.

Key question 3.3 ?

1 **Describe** two methods to ensure quality.
2 **Explain** two benefits of *each* method described in key question 1 above.

Ethical and environmental issues

* ★ Ethical operations
* ★ Environmentally friendly operations

Operations, in conjunction with the marketing department, need to consider how their products impact on **ethics** and the **environment**. By ensuring both are considered, an organisation will ensure they meet the **CSR** objectives (see page 11).

Ethical issues

Organisations should try to be **ethical**. This means they show moral consideration for others when making decisions.

Table 3.19 Advantages and disadvantages of being ethical

Advantages	Disadvantages
Awards can be granted for being ethical, which can be used for promotional purposes.	Audits are needed to ensure standards are met and maintained, which may be time consuming.
Businesses with an ethical reputation can attract customers and quality staff who agree with their principles.	Decision-making could be more complex and time consuming as many possible solutions may not be appropriate because they are not ethical.

Philanthropy

Philanthropy means having a 'love for humanity'. In other words, giving to those in need. This could be through charitable donations, giving away goods or setting up a charitable trust as part of the organisation.

Animal welfare

The moral considerations of an organisation need not only refer to how people are treated; increasingly these concerns are also around the treatment and wellbeing of animals. This might include the conditions that animals are kept in, the way they are handled, animal testing and the use of animal-derived ingredients.

Examples of ways that organisations can prove their commitment to animal welfare include:

* The 'leaping bunny' symbol awarded to products that are entirely cruelty free.
* The free range classification of eggs and egg-derived products.
* The use of synthetic materials rather than leather, fur or wool.

Figure 3.9 The Leaping Bunny logo is awarded to companies whose products and ingredients comply with the gold standard for no animal testing

Fair trade

Fair trade is when suppliers of raw materials receive a guaranteed and fair price for their goods. Fair trade also ensures that employees in the supply chain are treated fairly.

Organisations are encouraged to use suppliers that are part of the Fairtrade Foundation.

www

Find out more about how businesses can get involved with fair trade: **www.fairtrade.org.uk/ en/for-business**

Table 3.20 Advantages and disadvantages of fair trade

Advantages	Disadvantages
Businesses are awarded the Fairtrade mark on their products, which can appeal to customers.	Losing a Fairtrade mark after gaining one will result in bad publicity.
Stocking fair trade goods demonstrates the retailer's ethical commitment to its customers.	Fair trade products are often more expensive.
Businesses that are fair trade have a positive impact on the producers of the raw materials with which they work and have a better relationship with the supply chain.	The business has a more limited choice of suppliers.

Environmental issues

Organisations should do their bit to help the environment. This will have the following advantages and disadvantages.

Table 3.21 Advantages and disadvantages of being environmentally friendly

Advantages	Disadvantages
The organisation plays a part in looking after the environment that will hopefully sustain their activities for the future.	Investment in environmentally friendly measures will be expensive in the short term, e.g. installing solar panels.
Having a positive effect on the environment will ensure the organisation gains a positive reputation.	New procedures may have to be adapted to be more environmentally friendly, which can take time.
Awards can be granted for being 'environmentally friendly', which can be used for promotional purposes.	Most environmentally friendly procedures rely on the natural environment, which may not be sufficient, e.g. lack of wind, solar energy, etc.
Renewable energies save costs in the long run as fuels such as oil, petrol or gas don't need to be paid for.	

Carbon footprint

This refers to the impact that using fossil fuels, such as oil and gas, has on the environment. Examples of ways that organisations can prove their commitment to reducing their carbon footprint are:

- using alternative sources of 'renewable' energy, such as solar and wind, for example to power premises.
- using low emissions vehicles or EVs (electric vehicles) for deliveries and company cars.
- using altogether more environmentally friendly **methods of distribution** can be used (see page 85).

Sustainable raw materials

Being **sustainable** refers to ensuring that the raw materials used by a business activity are not being depleted. As well as respecting the natural environment and gaining a good reputation, this will ensure that businesses can source raw materials in the future.

Examples of ways that organisations can prove their commitment to this are:

- **replanting** raw materials that are used in production; for example, Velvet, the toilet roll brand, ran a successful campaign to replant 3 trees for 1 used until they reached a milestone of 10 million new trees planted!
- **reusing** or **recycling** materials to be used in production
- **sustainable resources**, for example, sustainable fishing limits the amount of fish that can be caught in an area to allow the fish to breed and naturally replenish. Businesses that can prove they use sustainable fish are awarded the MSC sustainable seafood logo
- **utilising renewable energies**.

Figure 3.10 Birdseye packaging showing the sustainably caught fish logo awarded by the Marine Stewardship Council (MSC)

Waste

Not only does committing to dealing with **waste** appropriately help the environment, it is a *legal responsibility* to store, transport and dispose of waste without harming the environment.

Organisations must ensure they comply with the following **duty of care** when dealing with waste:

- **segregate** waste appropriately, for example, keeping apart chemicals that may react
- **store** waste appropriately, for example, securing waste
- **transport** waste appropriately and securely.

Packaging

As well as being part of good **PR**, the packaging of products should be designed to be as environmentally friendly as possible. The 'green' qualities of packaging can even be promoted to help the product gain a good image.

Ways that packaging could be environmentally friendly include:

- being **reusable**. This means the packaging can be used again in its current format, for example, 'bags for life' or Barr's glass bottles being re-filled and sold again.
- being **recyclable**. This means the packaging can be recycled easily into something else, saving the use of fresh raw materials, for example, Lush recycle their plastic containers into scarves.
- being **biodegradable**. This means used packaging can break down more easily. The least biodegradable packaging is hard plastic bottle caps which can take up to 400 years to decompose! Many businesses are now replacing plastic straws with paper ones, which of course is good PR!

Case study 3.4
SEPA

The **Scottish Environment Protection Agency** (SEPA) is a public sector organisation that helps businesses protect and improve the environment to create health and wellbeing benefits, and economic success. SEPA offers guidelines on the following environmental responsibilities on its website:

- water pollution (e.g. discharges to rivers from factories)
- air pollution (e.g. airborne pollution caused by industry)
- waste storage, treatment and disposal (e.g. illegal fly tipping)
- land contamination (e.g. previous industrial use such as leaks and spills of oil)
- natural resources (e.g. overuse of fossil fuels)

Terry A'Hearn, SEPA Chief Executive, says of business's attitude to environmental issues: 'Poor leaders are going to pretend it isn't a problem, good leaders will face the reality of the situation. Only great leaders will understand that it is an opportunity for their businesses and organisations.'

SEPA suggests that businesses that follow its guidelines will reap the following benefits:

- Improved efficiency and productivity as a result of building a sustainable business
- Reductions in water, carbon-based energy, materials and waste use and associated expenses
- An improved reputation with staff, customers, suppliers and the public
- Increased market value through environmental sustainability
- An increase in the chance of funding as a result of demonstrating environmental performance
- Improved legal compliance, less chance of prosecution and fewer time-consuming visits from environmental regulators

Discussion points

In pairs, groups or on your own:

1 Suggest ways businesses could comply with the main environmental responsibilities outlined by SEPA.
2 Explain the benefits to a business of following SEPA guidelines.
3 Explain the costs to a business of not taking SEPA guidelines on board.

WWW

Find out more about what SEPA do by logging on to:
www.sepa.org.uk

Quick questions 3.4

1 Discuss one advantage and one disadvantage of using Fairtrade certified suppliers.
2 Describe two ways in which a business can reduce its carbon footprint.
3 Suggest three ways in which a business can ensure its packaging is environmentally friendly.

Use of technology in operations

Here is a summary of how technology can be used in the operations function.

- IT, for example laptops/tablets/smartphones and email, can be used to purchase supplies quickly.
- The internet can be used to research supplier prices.
- EPOS can be used with computerised inventory control to automatically re-order depleted inventory.
- Computerised devices can be used by warehouse staff to check and find inventory.
- Automated systems can track deliveries for both the business's and the customer's information.
- Spreadsheets can be used to accurately and quickly produce production budgets.
- CAM (computer aided manufacture), such as robotics, can be used in automated production.
- Emerging technologies such as solar energy, wind energy and EV can be used to harness renewable energy.

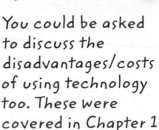

Remember

You could be asked to discuss the disadvantages/costs of using technology too. These were covered in Chapter 1 on page 30.

Key question 3.4

Describe how two types of technology are used in the operations function.

Exam-style questions practice – Chapter 3

1 Explain the advantages of including the following features in an inventory management control system:
   o Re-order quantity
   o Minimum inventory level
   o Buffer inventory. **(3 marks)**
2 Justify the use of just-in-time (JIT) inventory control. **(4 marks)**
3 Explain factors that will be considered when setting a minimum inventory level. **(3 marks)**
4 Describe the advantages of a business outsourcing its logistics management of inventory. **(5 marks)**
5 Describe the advantages to a large multinational of using centralised warehouses to store materials. **(4 marks)**
6 Compare the following:
   a) Capital intensive and labour intensive
   b) Mechanisation and automation. **(4 marks)**
7 Describe reasons for the method of production chosen by a manufacturer. **(3 marks)**
8 **a)** Discuss the advantages and disadvantages of quality circles. **(5 marks)**
   b) Describe other methods of ensuring quality. **(3 marks)**
9 Explain the ways an operations department can achieve the ethical and environmental considerations of a positive corporate social responsibility (CSR) policy. **(5 marks)**
10 Justify the use of spreadsheets in the operations department. **(2 marks)**

Chapter 4 Management of people

Workforce planning

What you should know

★ Elements of workforce planning
★ Internal and external supply of staff
★ Costs and benefits of selection methods

Reasons for workforce changes

New staff may be needed for the following reasons:
● to meet increasing demand for existing products
● to develop new products to satisfy demand
● to assist in opening new stores/factories
● to help enter new markets
● to respond to flexible working arrangements.

Existing staff may be removed or leave for the following reasons:
● to respond to falling sales/demand for products
● to take up positions with competitors or other local employers
● because employees retire, take sick leave, go on maternity leave, and so on
● the business needs different employees with new skills.

Steps in workforce planning

Workforce planning is about deciding how many and what types of workers are required and when. There are several steps involved in workforce planning:

1 The organisation analyses the potential demand for its goods/services and decides how many staff are needed and what skills are required to meet this demand. The organisation will take PESTEC factors into account (see Topic 5).

2 The organisation will conduct a **staffing forecast** to highlight if any staff are due to leave (maternity leave, retiring, etc.) and if there is a shortfall or surplus of staff.

3   The organisation analyses the profile of its current workforce to determine the need for new staff and the skills that need to be developed in existing staff.

4   If there is a surplus of staff then they may have to be removed; if there is a shortfall then the organisation 'closes the gaps' to ensure that it has the workforce required to provide the goods/services to meet their objectives by:
   a) recruiting and selecting new staff
   b) training existing staff
   c) retaining existing staff through motivation methods.

5   Review process and make changes if necessary.

Figure 4.1 Workforce planning cycle

Internal or external supply of staff?

An organisation can recruit for staff from either within the organisation (internal) or from outside the organisation (external).

Table 4.1 gives examples of where an organisation may advertise for each.

Table 4.1 Examples of job advertising methods

Internal	External
Staff noticeboard	Job centre
Organisation's intranet	Newspaper adverts
Internal email to all or selected staff	Websites such as Monster or S1 Jobs
Company newsletter	Recruitment agencies – specialist organisations that are experts in recruiting and selecting the best staff for other organisations. This is an example of outsourcing (see Topic 4).

Internal supply of staff

Table 4.2 Advantages and disadvantages of internal recruitment

Advantages	Disadvantages
The vacancy can be filled quickly.	Applicants are drawn from a very limited pool so the organisation may not hire the *best* person for the job.
The employee knows the organisation which saves induction training costs and time.	Promoting one employee will consequentially create a vacancy in their old post.
The employee is known to the organisation and can be trusted to do a good job.	The organisation misses out on a chance to bring in fresh, new ideas and new skills to the organisation.
The organisation saves money on external advertisement costs.	Employees can resent a fellow colleague being promoted over them. This can cause conflict and relations to become strained.
Employees will be more motivated as they know there is a chance of promotion.	

External supply of staff

Table 4.3 Advantages and disadvantages of external recruitment

Advantages	Disadvantages
Fresh, new ideas and skills are brought into the organisation.	Candidates do not know the organisation so induction training will have to be carried out, taking up production time and costing money.
There is a wider pool of candidates to choose from.	Such a potentially vast pool of candidates can mean it takes longer to choose suitable applicants for interview.
It avoids creating a further vacancy in the organisation.	The organisation does not know the successful candidate, which carries a risk that they may not be suited for the job, or worse are untrustworthy.
It avoids the jealousy and resistance that is often created by one employee being promoted over others.	Existing staff may be demotivated as they perceive that there is no chance of internal promotion.

Selection methods

Selection is the process of choosing the correct person from the pool of applicants that have applied for the job.

1 **Application forms and CVs**. An application form is a document, produced by the employer, containing questions that applicants answer to provide details of their skills, experience and qualities. This is often more useful than a **curriculum vitae (CV)**, which is usually a two page document listing a person's work experience, qualifications and personal experiences. By using an application form, every applicant answers the same questions, making it easier to compare their answers with those of another applicant than with a CV.

2 **Interviews**. All interviews are designed to compare the applicant's responses to questions against set criteria. Interviews can take various forms: with one manager (**one-to-one**), with a single manager, one manager after another (**successive**) or in front of a number of people at the same time (**panel**).

Table 4.4 Advantages and disadvantages of interviews

Advantages	Disadvantages
Interviews find out how an applicant reacts under pressure.	Some applicants can train specifically for interviews and say what the interviewers want to hear but may not be the best person for the job.
Interviews give an indication of the applicant's personality and character.	Interviews can be highly stressful. This means an organisation may miss out on quality employees who underperform in the pressure of an interview.

3 **Testing**. Tests provide additional information about an applicant; however, there are disadvantages.

Disadvantages of testing

- They can be time consuming to carry out
- They may put applicants under too much pressure to perform as they would once they get the job
- Candidates may be more prepared on the day and once hired not perform to the same levels evident in the test.

Table 4.5 contains possible tests an organisation can carry out.

Table 4.5 Tests used during selection

Attainment test	This allows an applicant to demonstrate their skills, e.g. ICT skills by completing a typing test. Performance of candidates can be directly compared.
Aptitude test	This assesses if a candidate has the natural abilities and personal skills for the job, e.g. a prospective customer services assistant roleplaying a scenario with an angry customer.
Psychometric test	This assesses an applicant's personality and mental suitability for a job. There are no right or wrong answers; instead, the test gives an insight into how an applicant thinks and if they would fit into the organisation.
Intelligence/IQ test	This measures a candidate's mental ability; used for jobs where candidates may be solving problems.
Medical test	This measures physical fitness levels which may be required for certain jobs, e.g. the fire service, armed forces, etc.

4 **Assessment centres**. Organisations use assessment centres to see a large number of applicants at the same time. Applicants take part in a variety of team-building and role-play exercises as well as a number of tests. This allows an organisation to scrutinise applicants, to assess their suitability for the job, as well as how they interact with others.

Table 4.6 Advantages and disadvantages of assessment centres

Advantages	Disadvantages
Allows an organisation to really scrutinise applicants over a longer period of time.	A venue will need to be hired, if an organisation doesn't have its own assessment centre, which is expensive.
Assesses how applicants interact with others.	Several managers will need to be sent to the centre to conduct and supervise the tests, losing production time.
Assesses how applicants react to role-play scenarios that mimic real work situations.	Such tests require careful planning and preparation, all of which takes time.
Reduces the chance of interviewer bias as the results are a true reflection of each applicant's abilities and not just what one manager thinks.	

5 **References**. This is using references, or information from referees. These are used to confirm that the candidate is who they say they are, and that they are reliable. References are usually requested from previous employers and/or someone else with authority, such as the head teacher at the candidate's school.
6 **Trial periods**. This involves an applicant being employed for a short period of time, a day, a week or longer, before they are offered the position permanently, to make sure they are capable of doing the job, and that they are reliable and trustworthy. This avoids an organisation making a mistake by offering a job to someone who isn't suitable, and potentially having to go through lengthy **discipline** and **dismissal** procedures.

Remember

A 'selection process' could include ALL of these selection methods. It **doesn't** include anything from the 'recruitment' process (e.g. Job Analysis) that you may have studied at N5.

Quick questions 4.1

1 Describe two reasons for workforce planning.
2 Suggest three steps involved in workforce planning.
3 Outline two advantages of promoting staff from inside the organisation.
4 Justify the use of trial periods to select staff.
5 Describe two features of assessment centres.

Topic 22

Training and development

Training means to improve the skills or knowledge of staff within an organisation. Table 4.7 lists the general advantages and disadvantages of training.

Table 4.7 The general advantages and disadvantages of training

Advantages	Disadvantages
It helps to improve the quality of products/service as employees have better skills.	It can be costly to an organisation if outside training centres or trainers are used.
It is motivational for staff as it makes them more confident to do their job and they feel the business is interested in developing them.	It can lead to lost production time.
It can be used to develop skills to cope with change in an organisation, such as the introduction of new technology.	Staff may leave after being trained.
It reduces the number of workplace accidents since staff are more aware of procedures.	Staff may be in a position to command higher wages once better skilled.
A good training programme can attract high-quality staff.	

Ways of training staff

The human resources department must ensure that staff develop their skills and knowledge. Not only will this motivate staff, as they will feel the organisation is taking an interest in developing them, but staff will also be more capable, productive and able to adapt to changing external factors. All staff should do some **continued professional development (CPD)** each year to enhance their skills and knowledge. Staff can be sent on training courses, take part in training days at work, carry out professional reading or use one of the following ways of training staff.

Corporate training schemes

Organisations can offer staff the chance to take part in **corporate training schemes**. These are intense programmes of training that will equip staff with enhanced skills so they are in a good position either for a pay rise or for a promotion, for example, through a management training scheme.

Case study 4.1
Vue

Vue cinemas have a **management training scheme** in place that allows employees to work their way up through the various levels in the management structure. Vue cinemas have a centralised structure, with the head office in London, while each division is grouped by location, with cinemas all over the UK, for example, in Glasgow, Edinburgh, Stirling and Aberdeen. A typical employee starts off working as a customer assistant at a local cinema and, if they show promise, can be placed on a management training scheme. Employees on the scheme attend training courses and have to prove they have met the learning objectives of each course at their **appraisals** with their line manager. Once their manager has agreed that they have met the objectives, they can be promoted to a team leader position and, eventually, to a manager or even a general manager position.

Discussion points

In pairs, groups or on your own, consider:

1   Why would a training scheme such as Vue's motivate staff?
2   Do you know of any other organisations that provide management training schemes? If not, take some time to use the internet to find some.

Table 4.8 Advantages and disadvantages of corporate training schemes

Advantages	Disadvantages
The organisation benefits from highly skilled staff.	Work time can be lost throughout the training.
Staff are motivated, which lowers staff turnover.	The organisation will have to pay staff more after training is complete.

Graduate training schemes are offered to university graduates who typically attain a 2.1 (the university version of a 'B') or above. Graduates are given an attractive starting salary and placed on an intense one- to three-year period of a mixture of work-based training and learning on the job at training centres.

Table 4.9 Advantages and disadvantages of graduate training schemes

Advantages	Disadvantages
Graduates are raw talent that can be moulded to learn the skills and knowledge specific to the industry/business.	Graduates command higher salaries than staff without degrees.
The attractive salary, benefits and promotion opportunities are motivational to graduates.	The schemes often have to unpick irrelevant university knowledge and re-teach 'real world' business.
Successful completion of the programme can lead to a full-time position.	Not all graduates on the programme are guaranteed full-time jobs, increasing staff turnover and impacting on morale.

Work-based qualifications

Organisations can also offer staff the chance to gain formal qualifications while working. In Scotland many of the qualifications are based on the SVQ (Scottish Vocational Qualifications) framework. SVQs are work-related qualifications that reflect the skills and knowledge required to do a specific job. This qualification can be achieved through an **apprenticeship** scheme. This is common in manual trades, such as joinery or plumbing, and they are mostly delivered in the workplace with some days spent at a local college when required.

Professional qualifications such as accounting or engineering examinations can also be studied for through work-based training.

Table 4.10 Advantages and disadvantages of work-based training and apprenticeships

Advantages	Disadvantages
Employees gain a recognised qualification and learn through practical application of their learning.	Staff may leave for a better job after gaining their qualification.
Employees can contribute to the organisation while training.	Organisations usually pay for the training and examinations.
Employees are paid during training which can be motivational.	It can be costly to pay staff to train.

Appraisals

An **appraisal** is a two-way meeting between an employee and another member of staff to discuss the employee's performance and to set targets for the future. An appraisal is traditionally a **formal** one-to-one meeting between an employee and their line manager; however, modern methods include **peer appraisal**, **360-degree appraisal** and informal appraisal which is just a quick chat with a subordinate, perhaps during a coffee break.

Table 4.11 Advantages and disadvantages of appraisals

Advantages	Disadvantages
Positive feedback can be given which motivates the employee.	Negative feedback can be given which demotivates employees.
Targets will be set for the employee which motivates them and gives them a goal to work towards.	An employee might be set unrealistic targets which puts them under pressure.
Training needs can be identified which can motivate staff and increase quality standards.	Too many development needs may be identified which will stress the employee.
Pay rises and bonuses can be awarded after a successful appraisal which will motivate staff and ensure their work rate improves further.	Some employees resent the appraisal system. They feel under pressure and as if they are being checked up on.
Employees can be identified for promotion, which will increase their loyalty to the organisation.	Appraisals are time consuming to carry out which will result in lost work time during the time they are being conducted.
Strong relationships are formed between managers and employees as they are given the opportunity to have a professional discussion.	

Peer appraisal

A peer appraisal is when the review interview is carried out by a colleague at the same level in the organisation as the employee.

Table 4.12 Advantages and disadvantages of peer appraisals

Advantages	Disadvantages
Employees may relax more and react better to a review given by a colleague.	Personal relationships between peers could result in the appraisal being ineffective.
Relationships with line managers are not harmed through judgements or weaknesses being highlighted.	Bias could wrongly highlight an employee for a pay rise or promotion.

360-degree appraisal

The most complete method is the 360-degree appraisal. In this scenario, whoever conducts the appraisal, such as an HR manager, peer or line manager, interviews fellow employees, supervisors and subordinates about the performance of the employee.

Figure 4.2 A 360-degree appraisal offers performance feedback from many different people

Table 4.13 Advantages and disadvantages of 360-degree appraisals

Advantages	Disadvantages
A complete profile of the employee is gained.	Some employees may find it difficult to be critical of their colleagues.
Areas of subjectivity, such as character and leadership skills, are measured.	Time constraints can limit the quality of responses from so many people in the organisation.

Quick questions 4.2

1 Describe two benefits of apprenticeship schemes.
2 Justify the use of a graduate training scheme.
3 Outline two advantages of training and development for employees.
4 Describe a 360-degree appraisal.
5 Suggest two ways in which an employee can carry out CPD.

Key question 4.1

Describe two approaches that could be used to manage human resources effectively.

Topic 23
Motivation and leadership

What you should know

★ Motivation theories
★ Role of management in motivating employees
★ Benefits of motivation
★ Leadership styles

Motivation theories

You read in Topic 9 about management theorist Henri Fayol's work, describing the role that managers have in organisations. We will now explore the theories of two more management theorists to gain an understanding of what motivates employees.

Maslow's hierarchy of needs

In 1943, Abraham **Maslow** said that humans had five sets of needs (motivators), which come in a particular order. As each level of needs is satisfied, the desire (motivation) to fulfil the next set kicks in. Everyone starts with the lowest, most basic need and works up until the highest need is reached. A person will not be motivated by the higher needs until their basic needs are met. Maslow's hierarchy is best illustrated as a pyramid (see Figure 4.3).

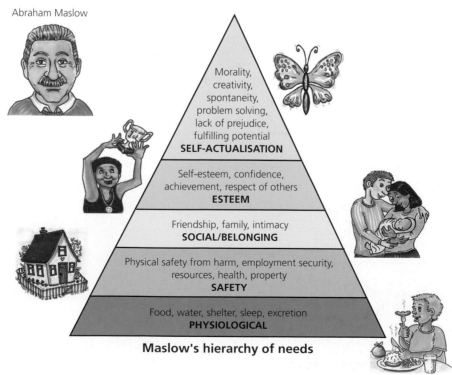

Abraham Maslow

Morality, creativity, spontaneity, problem solving, lack of prejudice, fulfilling potential
SELF-ACTUALISATION

Self-esteem, confidence, achievement, respect of others
ESTEEM

Friendship, family, intimacy
SOCIAL/BELONGING

Physical safety from harm, employment security, resources, health, property
SAFETY

Food, water, shelter, sleep, excretion
PHYSIOLOGICAL

Maslow's hierarchy of needs

Figure 4.3 Maslow's hierarchy of needs

Table 4.14 Implications of Maslow's hierarchy of needs for motivating staff

Need	Description	Implications for motivating staff
5 Self-actualisation	To realise potential and have status in life. Maslow wrote: 'What a man can be, he must be.'	Opportunities for creativity and personal growth, promotion opportunities.
4 Self-esteem	To feel worthy and respected.	A job title that stands out from others, recognition of one's achievements in front of peers.
3 Love and belonging	To fulfil social needs such as friendship and family.	A good team atmosphere, open plan offices, friendly supervision.
2 Safety and security	To feel safe at work, at home, financially and physically.	Safe working conditions, job security, fair wage rises in line with inflation.
1 Physiological needs	The basic needs for bodily functioning and staying alive; fulfilled by eating, drinking and going to the toilet.	A living wage, basic safe working environment, access to toilet facilities and running water.

Herzberg's motivator–hygiene theory

In 1959, Frederick **Herzberg** wrote the motivator–hygiene theory (also known as the two-factor theory) of motivation. According to Herzberg employees are motivated by two sets of factors: motivator factors and hygiene factors.

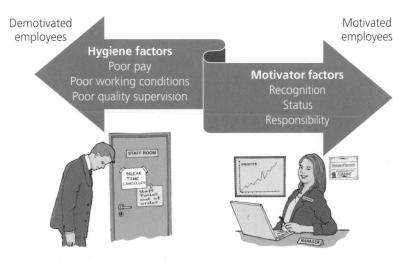

Figure 4.4 Herzberg's theory of motivation

Hygiene factors

Hygiene factors will not motivate employees, but if they are not met, they can *lower* motivation. These factors could be anything from clean toilets, lunch breaks and a break room, to a reasonable level of pay, job security, and supervision, procedures and policies that employees are happy with.

Motivator factors

Motivator factors will not necessarily lower motivation if they are absent or not used, but can be responsible for *increasing* motivation. These factors are also linked to the needs at the top of Maslow's hierarchy and could involve rewarding employees with status and recognition, potential for promotion and delegated responsibility.

Role of managers in motivating staff

Herzberg suggested that it is the role of managers to provide the **motivators** (to **satisfy** employees). They should give staff promotion opportunities, profit sharing schemes, recognition and challenges.

Herzberg also suggested that it is the role of managers to ensure the **hygiene factors** are ALL present (to avoid **dissatisfaction**). If any one of clean toilets, lunch breaks, fair pay, job security or basic safety are missing then employees will be demotivated.

Basic motivation methods

Management can use the different management theories to attempt to motivate staff through a number of basic methods.

Table 4.15 Basic motivation methods

Motivation method	How it motivates employees
Fair pay	Employees work to earn money to satisfy their needs and wants. If they don't think they are receiving a fair amount of pay for their work they will be demotivated and their productivity will decrease.
Payment methods	Organisations can use a number of payment methods to motivate staff: **Commission** – Salespeople can be offered commission, which is a percentage of the sales they make, motivating them to sell more. **PRP** – Performance-related pay, sometimes called a 'bonus', this is an extra payment on top of the basic wage for meeting agreed targets. **Piece rate** – The employee is paid per item they produce, which encourages a high work rate; however, the quality of work may drop. **Overtime** – When an employee works longer than their contractual hours, normally at a higher rate of pay, this encourages extra production to meet demand.
Incentives	Non-financial incentives could be offered, e.g. holidays, cars, discounts and private healthcare.
Permanent contracts	Employees need to feel that they have job security. Organisations should avoid the use of temporary contracts where possible. Permanent contracts will make employees feel more secure and they will get on with their jobs.
Good working conditions	Employees need to feel that their working conditions are safe. As Herzberg states, good working conditions won't necessarily motivate employees but bad working conditions will demotivate them. However, an improvement in working conditions, such as better equipment, a new office or company car may motivate staff for a short while.

Advanced motivation methods

Some employees will need more than a contract, pay and good conditions to be motivated at work. Organisations need to find ways to satisfy Herzberg's 'motivator' factors and meet Maslow's top two hierarchy needs too!

Table 4.16 Advanced motivation methods

Motivation method	How it motivates employees
Staff appraisals	Regular meetings with a manager are known as appraisals. These motivate employees as they are told what they are doing well and given targets to aim for. They can also be targeted for promotion.
Recognition	Employees who want to progress in their career respond well to recognition, such as an 'employee of the month scheme'.
Development opportunities	Employees will want to develop their skills, for example through a management training scheme, so they are able to be identified for promotion opportunities and improve their status in the organisation.
Empowerment	Empowerment means giving staff the authority to make their own decisions. Managers can delegate part of their responsibility to an employee and let them decide how best to carry it out. This will give employees a sense of job satisfaction.

Case study 4.2

Starbucks

The CEO of Starbucks, Howard Schultz, considers that the reason for Starbucks' success is not coffee but employees. The managers in Starbucks treat each employee equally and all of the staff are called 'partners', even the supervisors. In order to narrow the gap between managers and employees, managers also co-work with the lowest level of staff in the front line. Due to this, they can maintain good relations and create a much closer and friendlier atmosphere than other workplaces. Not only do employees enjoy their jobs but customers are also affected by their enthusiasm. Such an enthusiastic and vibrant atmosphere is key to the culture of Starbucks. It's even in their mission statement, to 'inspire the human spirit', and employees can be recognised for capturing the spirit in their work by being given the 'Spirit of Starbucks Award'. Starbucks managers have regular, informal appraisals with each employee, which can just be a quick chat, to ask them how they are doing and if they (the manager/organisation) can meet the employee's needs or even just to ask if they need a day off! Employees can also be sent on college courses to gain qualifications.

Employees are also asked to participate in quality circles and to let management know if they have a good idea, from a quick operational solution to a major strategic change. All employees are offered a great deal of incentives, for instance, discounts on Starbucks' products and medical insurance. They also have their own share–save scheme, called 'Bean Stock', to allocate stock dividends to all employees. Because of this, all managers and employees have the same goal; they are motivated to increase sales to earn more profit.

Discussion points

In pairs, groups or on your own:

1 Identify five methods Starbucks uses to motivate employees.
2 Consider which motivation method would motivate you or your group the most and why.
3 Consider which of the Starbucks motivation methods are motivator factors, according to Herzberg.

Benefits of motivating staff

- Increased productivity from employees
- Better quality products
- Better standard of customer service
- Reduced staff absenteeism and poor time-keeping
- Reduced staff turnover, reducing re-hiring costs
- Improved employee relations and fewer grievances

Remember

As with many topics you can apply the opposite of these benefits if asked about the effects of demotivated staff!

Leadership styles

Employees respond well to different managers. This is because all managers have a different style of leadership. These styles are described in Table 4.17 below.

Table 4.17 Advantages and disadvantages of the different leadership styles

Leadership style	Advantages	Disadvantages
Autocratic: Authority and control is retained by the leader. Managers tell employees what to do.	There are clear expectations of what needs to be done. Decisions can be made quickly. This works well when the manager is the most skilled or knowledgeable in the team.	There's no opportunity for delegation or empowerment, demotivating some staff. There's a lack of creativity in decision-making as it is retained with senior management.
Democratic: Communication and employee participation are key. Managers let employees have a say in decision-making.	Employees feel motivated as they have a say in decision-making. The manager has the final say but employees can contribute, which can encourage creativity and help solve complex problems.	Mistakes can be made if workers are not skilled or experienced enough to participate in decision-making. Some employees can be less productive than they would be under an autocratic manager.
Laissez-faire: A rough translation of the French phrase 'laissez-faire' is 'let them be'. Managers with this style do exactly that, they don't issue instructions or supervise staff, they just let staff carry out their jobs.	Employees are highly empowered to make decisions and only seek manager's assistance when they need help, which motivates employees. This can create a very relaxed work environment.	Lack of direction can lead to objectives not being met. This can only work in highly professional environments where workers are self-motivated, such as technology companies or creative industries.

Scenarios affecting leadership style

- **The task**: A complex task, such as deciding on new company policy, will require more direction from management (autocratic); a creative task, such as designing new packaging, would benefit from a hands-off approach (laissez-faire).
- **Time available**: There may be little time to complete a project which means less time for discussion on how to achieve it, so a more autocratic style will be required.
- **Skills of staff**: Highly skilled and competent staff will need less supervision and direction, so a democratic approach will work.
- **Motivation of staff**: Highly motivated employees can be trusted to have the self-discipline to make their own decisions and complete tasks without instruction and supervision.
- **Leader's own personality**: Leaders may lack personable qualities and automatically lead in an autocratic style. Similarly they may be too friendly and nice to be autocratic!
- **Group size**: Democratic styles can lead to confusion if the number of staff in a group is too large. Large groups benefit from the clear direction of autocratic leadership.
- **Corporate culture**: The culture in an organisation can persuade managers to use specific styles; for example, an open and relaxed environment found in technology firms lends itself to a laissez-faire approach.
- **Availability of finance**: Democratic and laissez-faire styles can delegate spending to departments and individuals. A lack of finance may lead to autocratic styles being adopted in order to control spending.

Quick questions 4.3 ❓

1. Suggest three actions a manager could take to motivate staff.
2. Describe the two factors of Herzberg's theory.
3. Describe ways in which staff's needs can be met according to any two stages of Maslow's hierarchy.
4. Suggest three effects of a demotivated workforce.
5. Describe the democratic style of leadership.

Key question 4.2 ❓

Describe two approaches that could be used to motivate staff to improve effectiveness.

Topic 24
Employee relations

What you should know

- ★ Impact of positive and negative employee relations
- ★ Company policies and processes
- ★ External institutions
- ★ Employee participation

Employee relations refers to the relationships that exist between management and employees in an organisation. The quality of employee relations will result in the following impacts on the organisation:

Impact of positive employee relations

- Employees will have their chance to discuss changes or grievances so will feel happier and more secure in the workplace.
- Disputes are less likely to arise as the workers will have been consulted and understand why changes are necessary.
- The workforce will be committed to the organisation and will help ensure it meets its objectives.
- It will be easier to introduce change within the organisation as staff will be more flexible with suggestions from management.
- The organisation will gain a good image for treating its employees correctly and maintaining good employee relations. Customers, investors and potential employees might be attracted to the organisation.

Impact of negative employee relations

If employee relations are poor, an organisation can experience:

- poorer employee performance due to low morale
- increased staff turnover as employees leave for a better work environment
- increased staff absenteeism
- less co-operation of staff during periods of change
- an increase in grievances and discipline problems
- industrial action, for example, in extreme cases:
  Strike – employees stop working altogether
  Go slow – work at a slow rate to reduce productivity
  Work-to-rule – complete only the tasks and hours in contract.

Company policies and processes

Grievances

Grievances are concerns, problems or complaints raised by an employee. Examples could include working conditions, disputes between staff and changes being introduced.

The employee should raise these concerns with their manager. If a worker has a grievance against their manager, they should contact their HR department, their trade union or ACAS.

Grievances are best dealt with in this way:
- Solve them early to stop them escalating into formal disputes
- Managers should be trained to deal with grievances
- Employees should be encouraged to be open and honest
- Managers shouldn't blame or judge
- Managers should listen to concerns from the employee and seek a resolution.

Remember

An organisation dealing with grievances, discipline and dismissal in the correct manner is key to ensuring positive employee relations.

Discipline

Organisations should have **company policies** (rules) regarding employee conduct and set procedures in place to deal with employees who fail to follow them. These rules could cover: **absenteeism**, conduct and personal use of telephones and the internet.

The following would be an appropriate **disciplinary procedure**, should any of the above rules be breached.

1 Deal with cases of minor misconduct or unsatisfactory performance, or an employee's first breach of company policy informally. A quiet word is often all that is required to improve an employee's conduct or performance.
2 Employers should deal with issues promptly, fairly and consistently.
3 Where some form of formal action is needed, investigations should be carried out to gather and establish all the facts of the case.
4 Employees should be given the facts of the case and allowed to put their response forward.
5 Employees have the right to be accompanied to any formal disciplinary meeting (for example, by a trade union representative) and be allowed to appeal against any formal decision made on sanctions to be issued.

For minor offences, employees could escalate through these sanctions until the sanctions are exhausted; however, serious offences, such as theft from the organisation, could lead to immediate dismissal.

Dismissal

A dismissal is when an employer terminates the employee's contract. Dismissal should be the last resort in terms of sanctions for breaking company policy and should only be used after formal disciplinary procedures have taken place.
- Employers must be able to give account of the policies the employee has broken and the procedures and sanctions that have been used before dismissal.
- Employers should use a fair and consistent procedure when dismissing employees.
- Employees have a right not to be unfairly dismissed. Employers could contact ACAS for advice on what constitutes unfair dismissal, for example, dismissing a female employee for absence during pregnancy.

Remember

Sanctions could include:
- ☞ a formal written warning
- ☞ a final written warning, if it is a serious or repeat offence
- ☞ suspension of employment, with or without pay
- ☞ demotion
- ☞ dismissal.

Redundancy

Redundancy is when an employer feels that they no longer need an employee. It is usually a process that is carried out when a business needs to cut costs and other options have been explored. It is a last resort as redundancies bring about a very negative image for the business. Employers have to have a policy in place that will entitle those made redundant to a set notice period (to hopefully find another job) and a **redundancy payment**, often linked to years' service, for example, one week's wage for every year worked with the company.

External institutions

Often, employees need assistance from external institutions in order to come to agreements with their employers, especially if disputes occur.

Trade unions

A trade union is an organisation that represents a group of employees. Members benefit from the **collective bargaining** power of the trade union, the experience of the union leaders who represent them and the union (the power that comes from speaking as a group rather than as a number of individuals). This gives employees a stronger voice when negotiating pay rises or improvements in working conditions. Members of a trade union also benefit from the powers the union has should matters need to be taken to court. Examples of trade unions are shown in Figures 4.5 and 4.6.

Activity 4.1

Take a look at the website of the largest trade union in the UK www.unitetheunion.org and consider the tasks below. You can discuss the points or type up your findings.

1 Find out about all the different industries the union represents.
2 Find out about what different employees are fighting for.

ACAS

When a trade union cannot come to an agreement with an employer on behalf of its members, the organisation can involve ACAS. This is a government-funded organisation which attempts to solve disputes in the workplace to stop them going to court. ACAS stands for the Advisory, Conciliation and Arbitration Service.

- **Advisory**: ACAS are experts on all HR matters, such as legislation. ACAS can provide advice to organisations to help them understand HR policy and avoid disputes going further. ACAS also offers training to organisations. ACAS's belief is that 'prevention is better than cure'.

Figure 4.5 UNISON – union for public sector workers in health, education, local government, police, energy and the voluntary sector

Figure 4.6 Unite the union – the largest union in the UK, covering all industries such as finance, automotive and IT

WWW

Find out more about ACAS at the following website:
www.acas.org.uk

- **Conciliation**: A conciliator is similar to a referee. Conciliation involves an impartial ACAS conciliator discussing the dispute with both parties to help them reach a better understanding of each other's position and to reach an agreement before going to arbitration or court.
- **Arbitration**: An arbitrator (in this case ACAS) makes a final decision on a dispute, based on the evidence presented by both parties. Arbitration is voluntary, so both sides must agree to go to arbitration; they should also agree that they will stand by the arbitrator's decision. Arbitration by ACAS avoids matters going to court, which can be costly, take up many hours of work time and be stressful for both parties.

Employee participation

Organisations can utilise a variety of methods to involve employees in decision-making:

Worker-director – when a worker-director position is created, a low-level employee such as a factory worker or a sales assistant is given a seat on the Board of Directors. Worker-directors have no voting rights; however, they present their views and the views of fellow workers to the board. Ultimately, employees feel that they have a say in decision-making.

Works councils – are groups made up of an equal number of employees and managers. The group discusses major suggestions for change in the organisation and has joint decision-making powers. This reduces resistance to change from employees.

Consultative committees – are similar and can also include members of the public, customers, etc. to discuss important issues or changes.

Quality circles – (see page 94) involve employees being consulted on how to improve the standard of the products they produce. This makes employees feel involved in decision-making and that they can make a difference.

Case study 4.3

BMW

When BMW announced the launch of the new MINI they knew it would mean a major change to the procedures at their Oxford factory. They wanted to take the chance to improve employee relations and not let the change harm relationships and communication. Firstly, BMW consulted staff about the changes taking place in the factory. Employees from the factory floor made it clear that they wanted to work as a team *with* management on the new MINI project. So, secondly, BMW hired extremely experienced and talented managers to work on the project, which helped employees feel confident that those in authority knew what they were doing and were qualified to lead the team. Thirdly, each manager adopted a democratic leadership style, allowing all employees to have an input in decision-making. This employee participation helped foster a culture of teamwork at BMW. The results spoke for themselves too; absenteeism fell dramatically and the rate of production increased by 40 per cent.

$\Rightarrow$

⇨
Discussion points
In pairs, groups or on your own:

1 Consider what other methods of employee participation BMW could have used.
2 Consider the reasons why absenteeism dropped at BMW.
3 List all the methods BMW used to improve relations with employees. Why do you think they worked?

Quick questions 4.4

1 Suggest two disadvantages of redundancy for an organisation.
2 Outline two factors an organisation should consider when disciplining an employee.
3 Describe the role of the following external institutions:
   a) ACAS
   b) trade unions.
4 Describe the term 'grievance'.
5 Suggest three ways in which organisations can encourage employee participation.

Key question 4.3

Explain two ways employee relations can impact on the success of a large organisation.

Activity 4.2

A fun activity to revise the *Management of people* chapter is to produce an 'induction booklet' for an organisation of your choice. You could:

- use your own workplace, if you have a part-time job
- choose somewhere you *want* to work in the future! Most large business websites will have plenty of information on their HR department
- complete this activity using the workplace of a friend or family member, if you can't find out the information you need online.

Create the booklet in Microsoft Word, or on paper if you prefer, and include:

1 an introduction to the company and the recruitment/selection process
2 why it is great to work there. (This is where an employer shows off their positive employee relations, how they motivate staff and their 'corporate culture' to new staff!)
3 why training is important
4 methods of training:
   a) description of each method
   b) what each method includes (use real examples)
   c) the benefits – to the staff *and* to the organisation
   d) the costs to the business (to highlight how nice they are being)
5 grievance and discipline procedures.

Legislation

★ Impact of current employee legislation
★ Health and Safety at Work Act
★ Equality Act
★ National minimum wage/Living wage

Employment legislation

Legislation is the laws that are introduced by the government. It is the role of the human resources department to take account of employment legislation and ensure it is followed accurately and consistently within an organisation. Failure to follow legislation can impact an organisation in the following ways:

● Employee relations can be adversely affected.
● Employees can become demotivated.
● Legal action can be taken, which will affect productivity.
● The business can be fined.
● The business will have a poor public image.

Equality Act 2010

❏ **Replaces previous anti-discrimination laws** (e.g. Sex Discrimination Act) with a single act to make the law simpler and to remove inconsistencies.

❏ **The act covers nine protected characteristics** that cannot be used as a reason to treat people unfairly. Every person has one or more of the protected characteristics, so the act protects *everyone* against unfair treatment.
These are:
  ☞ Age, disability, gender, race, marriage status, pregnancy and maternity, religion or belief, sexual orientation and gender reassignment.

❏ **There are seven different types of discrimination** under the new legislation.
These are:
  ☞ Harassment – this is behaviour that is deemed offensive by the recipient due to a protected characteristic.
  ☞ Victimisation – this occurs when someone is treated badly because they have made or supported a grievance.
  ☞ Direct discrimination – where someone is treated less favourably than another person because of a protected characteristic, e.g. a job advertised as 'not for males'.
  ☞ Indirect discrimination – when a rule or policy applies to everyone but disadvantages a person with a protected characteristic, e.g. a promotion being for over 30s.
  ☞ Associative discrimination – discrimination against someone because they are associated with another person who possesses a protected characteristic.
  ☞ Discrimination by perception – thinking someone has a characteristic and discriminating against them.
  ☞ Harassment by a third party – employers are liable for the harassment of their staff or customers by people they don't themselves employ, e.g. when outsourcing part of the business.

Figure 4.7 Equality Act 2010

Remember

You don't need to know ALL 9 characteristics and ALL 7 types of discrimination but it will help to have a few of each up your sleeve.

National Minimum Wage and National Living Wage

- ❏ The **National Minimum Wage** (NMW) is the minimum pay per hour most workers under the age of 25 are entitled to by law.
- ❏ The government's **National Living Wage** (NLW) is the minimum pay per hour most workers aged 25 and over are entitled to by law.
- ❏ The rate will depend on a worker's age and if they are an **apprentice**.

Age of employee	Rate from March 2018
25 and over	£7.83
21 to 24	£7.38
18 to 20	£5.90
Under 18	£4.20
Apprentice*	£3.70

- It is against the law for employers to pay workers less than the NMW or NLW, or to falsify payment records.
- Employers must calculate work-related costs, such as renting tools or cleaning uniforms, and ensure employees are paid above the minimum wage after these costs are deducted.
- This act may conflict with the Equality Act and see a rise in the employment of young workers to reduce wage costs.
- Any increase to the minimum wage by the government will increase the costs to the business and lower profits.
- If an employer doesn't pay the correct rate, a worker could take out a grievance against their employer.
- If the situation cannot be resolved internally an employee could choose to make a complaint to an Employment Tribunal.
- Alternatively, HMRC can fine the business up to £20,000 per underpaid employee.

*You MUST use the word **NATIONAL** when referring to both the **National** Minimum and **National** Living Wage legislation.*

Figure 4.8 National Minimum Wage and National Living Wage

Remember

You need to know the impact of legislation on organisations.

Health and Safety at Work Act 1974

- ❏ It is the duty of every *employer* to ensure the health, safety and welfare at work of all employees, for example:
  - ☞ The provision and maintenance of machinery and equipment so they are safe and without risks to health.
  - ☞ The provision of training and instruction on safety issues, particularly regarding dangerous chemicals and equipment.
  - ☞ Employers should prepare a written statement of their general health and safety policy and ensure employees are aware of it, including any updates.
- ❏ Employees' duties include regarding care of their own and other employees' health and safety, such as reporting of incidences or accidents, for example.

Offices, Shops and Railway Premises Act 1963

- ❏ This is the original health and safety legislation that sets out more specific laws regarding safety at work, such as cleanliness, overcrowding, temperature, ventilation, lighting, toilet facilities, supply of drinking water, for example.

Figure 4.9 Health and Safety legislation

Take a look at government legislation in more detail at the official legislation website:
www.legislation.gov.uk

Use of technology in managing people

Here is a summary of how technology can be used in the human resources function.

- The internet can be used to advertise vacancies online, increasing the number of potential applicants.
- Video-conferencing can be used to interview applicants. This saves time and travel costs but allows body language and facial expressions to be analysed, as well as the applicant's general appearance to be seen, unlike telephone interviews.
- Email can be used to organise training or appraisals, allowing many employees to be contacted at once.
- E-diaries can be used, allowing meetings and appointments to be scheduled more easily. Subordinates can also see their superiors' e-diary, and vice versa, so that meetings can be arranged without clashes occurring.
- Virtual learning platforms can be used for training purposes.
- ICT, such as laptops and email, can allow employees to work away from the office.
- Online testing can be used to test a large number of candidates at once, without the need for travel, and they can be automatically marked.

Virtual learning

A virtual learning environment is a way to access learning and teaching tools, to help staff gain knowledge and training, through the internet. These are similar to the various 'e-learning' platforms you may have used in your school or college, such as Glow or Edmodo. Using a virtual learning environment, staff can access learning and assessment materials, submit assignments and even interact with other students and trainers via webcam. Staff can use virtual learning for any form of training, such as induction training, work-based qualifications or training schemes.

Table 4.18 Advantages and disadvantages of training using a virtual learning environment

Advantages	Disadvantages
Trainees can access materials from home or while travelling, and at any time of day.	Some trainees will be more reassured by face-to-face contact.
Trainees can interact with trainers through video-conferencing or chat facilities.	The virtual learning environment can be costly to set up.
Saves money on sending trainees to courses and on printing training materials.	There's no guarantee that staff will complete all the training in the virtual learning environment.

Quick questions 4.5 ?

1 Outline two benefits of interviewing candidates by video call, e.g. Skype.
2 Describe two disadvantages of virtual learning environments.
3 Identify three characteristics protected under the Equality Act 2010.
4 Outline two types of discrimination according to the Equality Act 2010.
5 Compare the National Living Wage with the National Minimum Wage.
6 Describe two employee duties according to the HASAWA.
7 Outline two impacts of an organisation not obeying legislation.

Key questions 4.4 ?

1 **Identify** a current employment legislation act.
2 **Describe** two effects of the law identified in question 1 on employees or the organisation.

Exam-style questions practice – Chapter 4

1 Discuss the advantages and disadvantages of external recruitment. **(6 marks)**
2 Discuss the use of attainment tests to select staff. **(5 marks)**
3 Describe steps involved in workforce planning. **(8 marks)**
4 a) Justify the use of corporate training schemes. **(2 marks)**
   b) Describe other ways of training staff while they contribute to the business. **(2 marks)**
5 Justify the use of the following methods of appraisal:
   a) 360 degree
   b) Peer to peer. **(2 marks)**
6 Describe the role of hygiene factors in motivating staff, according to Herzberg.
7 a) Describe factors that would affect the leadership style of a manager. **(5 marks)**
   b) Distinguish between the following leadership styles: autocratic and laissez-faire. **(2 marks)**
8 Explain the impact of negative employee relations on an organisation. **(4 marks)**
9 Justify three methods of employee participation. **(3 marks)**
10 Explain the disadvantages of using a virtual learning environment (VLE) to train staff. **(2 marks)**

Chapter 5 Management of finance

Sources of finance

What you should know

★ Sources of finance
★ Factors affecting sources of finance

Sources of finance

A business can be financed via a number of different sources and there are advantages and disadvantages to each source as shown in Table 5.1.

Hints & tips

*The finance chapter has always given many Higher Business Management students the fear, but don't think this! Make sure you revise finance because, although it is actually a very small section compared to others, it **must** still come up in the exam!*

Table 5.1 Advantages and disadvantages of different sources of finance

Source of finance	Advantages	Disadvantages
Owner's personal finance: Includes personal savings and money borrowed from family and friends.	This allows the owner to keep control of the business. It can reduce the amount to be borrowed from other sources.	It can be difficult to withdraw savings once they are invested in the business. There is a risk that the owner could lose their savings if the business fails.
Retained profits: A business holding back profits from previous years.	This can be used to make larger purchases, such as assets or for bulk buying. The business doesn't go into debt	A business can find it more difficult to grow if it regularly uses retained profits, especially to solve short-term cash-flow problems.
Sale of assets: Selling something that the business no longer needs.	Money can be raised from the sale of an asset to boost cash flow. The money does not need to be repaid.	If the finance is required urgently, the business may have to sell the asset for less than it is worth.

Source of finance	Advantages	Disadvantages
Sell and lease back: Selling an asset and leasing (renting) it back.	The use of the asset is retained, which might be essential to the business, e.g. selling and leasing back the main shop/factory/office. The business passes over responsibility for maintaining and renewing equipment to the leasing company.	Leasing over a long period of time can be expensive – ultimately, the business may pay back more than it received from the sale.
Share issue: Selling shares in the business. PLCs sell on the stock market. Ltds sell shares privately.	Very large sums of money can be raised through the sale of shares. The money does not need to be repaid.	Dividends have to be paid to shareholders. It can be expensive to advertise and organise the sale of shares.
Debentures: Loans borrowed from individuals through the stock market.	Control of the business is retained. These can be paid back over a long time.	Interest must be paid annually, even if a loss is made, unlike with shares where dividends are only paid out if profits are made.
Bank overdraft: A facility which allows a business to spend more money than is in its bank account.	This is usually easy for a business to arrange with its bank. It allows a business to continue to pay business expenses, despite there being no money in its bank account.	High interest rates are usually applied by the bank for borrowing money in this way. The overdraft can be withdrawn by the bank at any time and must then be repaid.
Trade credit: Allows a business to buy goods from suppliers and pay for them at a later date.	This allows a business to sell goods at a higher price and earn a profit before the bill needs to be paid. It helps a business to keep going when cash flow is poor.	Discount for prompt payment is lost. Suppliers will be reluctant to continue to offer credit if a business does not pay within the agreed credit period.
Debt factoring: A business sells its unpaid customer invoices to a factoring company. The factoring company then collects and keeps the customers' debts.	Responsibility for collecting the debt is passed on to the factor, saving the company time and effort. Cash flow is improved by receiving an advanced payment of the debts from the factor.	The business has to sell the customer debt for a reduced amount, i.e. it receives less money than is actually owed. Factoring companies are usually only interested in large amounts of debt.
Grants: Money is given to a business from central or local government, the EU or the Prince's Trust.	These are often offered as an incentive and a way of helping a business get started or expand. The money does not need to be repaid.	They can be complicated to apply for and can require the business to meet certain requirements. Grants are usually one-off payments that are not repeated.
Bank loan: A bank agrees to lend a business money for a specific purpose, for a fixed period of time. Regular repayment instalments are put in place.	The business can budget for the repayments. Purchases of essential equipment can be made in advance and paid back over a number of years.	Interest has to be repaid along with the loan amount. Small businesses may find it more difficult to secure a loan and often need to pay higher interest rates, as they are a greater risk.

Source of finance	Advantages	Disadvantages
Hire purchase: A business can buy an asset by paying an initial deposit and then monthly payments for a fixed period of time.	Expensive equipment can be bought with only an initial deposit. The asset, e.g. a delivery van, is owned by the business at the end of the repayment period.	The business does not own the asset until the last instalment is paid. It can be an expensive form of borrowing if interest rates are high.
Mortgage: A large sum of money borrowed from a bank or building society secured on a property.	It can be paid back over a long period of time, e.g. 25 years. The interest rate charged is often lower than the rate on a bank loan.	Interest has to be repaid along with the loan amount. The mortgage provider owns the property until the last repayment is made. This means the business could lose the property if it does not keep up the repayments.
Venture capitalists: Organisations that invest in established businesses in return for equity (ownership percentage).	Large amounts of investment can be gained. Venture capitalists are willing to take on more risky investments than banks.	Venture capitalists have an equity stake, which means control and a share of profits are given up.
Crowd-funding: Small amounts of money from a large number of people are raised to fund a new business or a project. This is typically done via the internet, e.g. Kickstarter.	Finance can be raised from individuals when banks see a venture as too risky. Some funds are donated, so there is nothing to repay.	There is a low success rate. Only a small percentage of crowd-funded ventures get off the ground, often because they have not reached their target amount. Privacy can be a problem as ideas become public and can therefore be copied.

Factors affecting sources of finance

The **sources of finance** selected by or available to a business will depend on a number of factors:

Table 5.2 Factors affecting sources of finance

Factor	Description
Short-term finance required	An organisation may only need finance for a short term, perhaps to cover a cash-flow problem, so an overdraft could be used.
Long-term finance required	An organisation may need long-term finance, perhaps to fund the purchase of property, so would choose a mortgage.
Interest rates	An organisation will choose the finance with the lowest interest rate available. Often a hire purchase agreement will have a lower interest rate than a bank loan so would be selected to keep the cost of the finance as low as possible.
Payback term	The quicker the payback term, the less interest the organisation will pay on borrowing.
Size and type of organisation	Organisations are restricted to certain sources of finance, for example, a public sector organisation cannot sell shares and has to rely on government funding.

Hints & tips

There are many sources of finance and that seems daunting, but make sure you learn as many as you can. It is a common topic area in the exam that you should aim to score well in.

Quick questions 5.1

1 Justify the use of hire purchase.
2 Describe the term 'crowd-funding'.
3 Describe one advantage and one disadvantage of debt factoring.
4 Suggest two places from which a business could obtain a grant.
5 A business needs funds for 60 days only. Suggest two appropriate sources of finance.

Key questions 5.1

1 **Describe** two sources of finance for a large organisation.
2 **Justify** your suggestions in key question 1 above.

Topic 27
Cash budgeting

What you should know

★ Purpose of budgeting
★ Interpretation and analysis of cash budgets
★ Cash-flow problems and solutions

Cash-flow problems and solutions

Cash budgets need to be prepared to help organisations remain **liquid**. Liquidity refers to the cash-flow situation in an organisation. Organisations need to remain liquid in order to have the funds to pay off their debts.

Purpose of budgeting

A cash budget is a financial statement used for the following reasons:
● to predict a positive cash-flow situation (**surplus**)
● to predict a negative cash-flow situation (**deficit**)
● to allow investment to be planned during a surplus
● to allow action to be taken to avoid a deficit
● to be compared with actual figures and used to measure the performances of individual departments or divisions.

In addition to arranging sources of finance, if an organisation encounters cash-flow problems from the following sources, there are various ways to solve them:

Table 5.3 Solutions to cash flow problems

Problem	Solution
Too much money tied up in inventory	Use just-in-time (JIT) inventory control (see pages 86–7). Sell off excess inventory, e.g. through a 'sale'.
Too many credit sales	Offer cash discounts to encourage customers to pay in cash.
Too long a payment period for credit sales	Charge higher interest on credit sales to encourage customers to pay sooner.
Not enough credit purchases	Switch suppliers to those with interest-free credit available on purchases.
High amounts of spending on non-current assets	Pay for non-current assets in instalments, such as paying for a vehicle using hire purchase.
Increasing expense costs	Look for ways to reduce expenses, e.g. spend less on rent by selling online through e-commerce.
Too many drawings by owners	Charge higher interest on drawings to discourage owners from withdrawing money from the business.
Not enough sales revenue	Adapt the marketing mix (see pages 63–6) to encourage more sales, e.g. lower prices.
Too many unpaid debts	Sell debts to debt factoring companies.

Interpretation and analysis of cash budgets

A cash budget is an internal document prepared for a business's own use *ahead of time*, i.e. it predicts what is likely to happen in terms of cash coming in, cash going out and the overall cash leftover. Table 5.4 describes the terms used in a cash budget.

Table 5.4 Terms that appear in a cash budget

Term	Definition
Opening balance	The amount of cash available at the start of the month.
Total receipts	The total cash received during the month.
Cash available	The amount of cash available to spend. Calculated by: **opening balance + total receipts**
Total payments	The total amount of cash spent during the month.
Closing balance	The amount of cash available at the end of the month. Calculated by: **cash available – total payments**

Example 5.1

Cash budget for Fir Park Ltd for 3 months Aug–Oct 20XX	£	£	£	£	£	£
	Aug		Sep		Oct	
Opening balance		1000		3800		450
Receipts						
Cash sales revenue	5000		4000		2800	
Loan	1000		–		–	
Total receipts		6000		4000		2800
Cash available		7000		7800		3250
Payments						
Purchases	1800		1900		2000	
Wages	800		800		800	
Rent	600		600		650	
Purchase of van	0		4000		0	
Loan interest	0		50		100	
Total payments		3200		7350		3550
Closing balance		3800		450		−300

> **Hints & tips** ★
>
> *Notice the opening balance is the closing balance from the previous month!*

The following interpretations can be made by analysing the information in the cash budget for Fir Park Ltd:

Table 5.5 Interpreting the cash budget of Fir Park Ltd

Problem	Interpretation	Solution
Cash sales are falling.	This could be caused by seasonal factors such as the business selling goods suitable for summer months only. There may also be other external factors at play, such as a recession or rising interest rates.	The business should engage in marketing activities, for example, lowering prices or launching promotions, such as advertising or buy-one-get-one-free (BOGOF) deals to encourage custom.
Purchases are increasing. .	The business is tying too much money up in inventory. The goods are not selling, yet they have ordered more and more.	Use just-in-time (JIT) inventory control or find a cheaper supplier.
Expenses are increasing.	The business is paying increasing costs for expenses, for example rising rent costs in October.	Switch to cheaper premises or sell online to cut rent costs dramatically.
Negative closing balance.	The business had a deficit in October which means their payments outweigh their receipts. This leaves the business unable to pay off other debts and expenses.	Arrange more finance in the short term, such as another loan, overdraft or attract investment, for example, through venture capital/business angels.

Case study 5.1

Clemod PLC

You have been given the following financial statement from Clemod PLC. Study the information and attempt the Discussion points below.

Cash Budget for Clemod PLC for 3 months Nov–Jan 20xx						
	£	£	£	£	£	£
	Nov		Dec		Jan	
Opening balance		500		750		?
Receipts						
Cash sales revenue	3000		4500		2000	
Loan	0		0		1000	
Total receipts		3000		4500		3000
Cash available		3500		5250		3580
Payments						
Purchases	1400		1800		1800	
Wages	800		800		800	
Rent	550		570		590	
Computer purchase	0		1500		0	
Loan interest	0		0		100	
Total payments		2750		4670		3290
Closing balance		750		580		290

Remember

Only **cash** sales appear in a cash budget. A business might make a lot of credit sales (known as trade receivables) but until the customers pay in cash the money won't show.

Discussion points

In pairs, groups or on your own:

1 Identify the opening balance for January.
2 Outline four sources of cash-flow problems faced by Clemod PLC.
3 Suggest solutions to the problems you have identified in the previous question.
4 Explain possible reasons for the increase in sales in December.

Quick questions 5.2 ?

1 Describe two reasons for preparing cash budgets.
2 Suggest two ways in which a business could encourage customers to pay in cash rather than credit.
3 Identify three items a business needs to pay for with cash.

Topic 28
Financial statements

Users of financial statements

Table 5.6 Users and purposes of financial statements

User	Purpose
Owners	To assess profits and to inform decision-making.
Employees	To ensure their jobs are secure.
HMRC	To ensure the business is paying the correct amount of tax.
Trade unions	To assess if their members are due a pay rise.
Competitors	To measure their success against each other.
Investors	To assess the potential for investment.
Lenders	To decide whether or not to give a loan.

Income statement

An **income statement** shows the profit made from buying and selling, known as **gross profit**, and the profit made after expenses are deducted from gross profit, known as **profit for the year**.

Table 5.7 defines the terms that appear in an income statement:

Table 5.7 Terms that appear in an income statement

Term	Definition
Sales revenue	The amount of money made from selling goods or services.
Cost of sales	The amount of money spent on selling goods. Calculated by: **(opening inventory + purchases) – closing inventory**
Gross profit	The profit made from buying and selling. Calculated by: **sales revenue – cost of sales**
Expenses	Running costs incurred throughout the year.
Profit for the year	The profit made after expenses are deducted from gross profit. Calculated by: **gross profit – expenses**

Example 5.2

Income statement for Auchmuty PLC for year ended 31 Dec 20XX		
	£000	£000
Sales revenue		1000
Less Cost of sales		
Opening inventory	50	
Add Purchases	250	
	300	
Less Closing inventory	25	
Cost of sales		275
Gross Profit		725
Less Expenses		
Wages	250	
Administration	100	
Advertising	75	425
Profit for the year		300

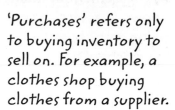

Remember

'Purchases' refers only to buying inventory to sell on. For example, a clothes shop buying clothes from a supplier.

Hints & tips ⭐

Note the use of the words Less (−) *and* Add (+) *in the income statement to indicate how the different totals are calculated.*

Case study 5.2

Lesmahagow Ltd

You have been given the following financial statement for Lesmahagow Ltd. Study the information and complete the Discussion points below.

Income statement for Lesmahagow Ltd for year 1 to year 3			
	Year 1	Year 2	Year 3
	£000	£000	£000
Sales revenue	5000	6000	8000
Less Cost of sales	2000	2100	2500
Gross profit	3000	3900	5500
Less Expenses	1500	1300	1600
Profit for the year	1500	2600	3900

Hints & tips ⭐

You don't need to be able to prepare these financial statements; however, you do need to be able to **interpret** *them. Understanding how the statements are calculated will help you do this.*

Discussion points

In pairs, groups or on your own:

1   Describe the trends in the following:
 a) profits
 b) expenses
 c) sales revenue.
2   Suggest possible reasons for the trends you described above.
3   Consider what would happen to the following in Year 4 if expenses increased by £200 and everything else remained constant:
 a) Profit for the year
 b) Gross profit.

Statement of financial position

The **statement of financial position** shows the items a business owns, known as **assets**, the items they owe, known as **liabilities**, and the overall **value** of the business. Table 5.8 defines the terms that appear in a statement of financial position:

Table 5.8 Terms that appear in a statement of financial position

Term	Definition
Non-current assets	Items owned for a period of more than one year.
Current assets	Items owned for a period of less than one year.
Current liabilities	Items owed for a period of less than one year.
Working equity	The ability to pay short-term debts. Calculated by: **current assets − current liabilities**
Net assets employed	This is the value of non-current assets added to the working equity figure (if positive − if working equity is negative it will be subtracted from non-current assets). Calculated by: **non-current assets +/− working equity**
Non-current liabilities	Long-term debts of the business, e.g. bank loan, debentures etc.
Net assets	The overall value or worth of the business. Calculated by: **net assets employed − non-current liabilities.**
Equity & Reserves	This shows how the business has been financed, e.g. the initial investments in the business (equity, shares, etc.), retained profits, etc. It should add up to the exact value of total net assets.

Example 5.3

Statement of financial position for Binos Ltd as at 31 Dec 20xx			
	£000	£000	£000
Non-current assets			
Premises			1500
Vehicles			175
Equipment			<u>100</u>
			1775
Add **Current assets**			
Closing inventory	25		
Trade receivables	<u>700</u>	725	
Less **Current liabilities**			
Bank overdraft	150		
Trade payables	<u>50</u>	200	
Working equity			<u>525</u>
Net assets employed			2300

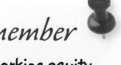

Remember

Trade payables are suppliers the business owes money to.
Trade receivables are customers that owe money to the business.

Remember

The **working equity** figure is very important. It states how much money the business has access to in the short term, to pay for debts and general running costs.

Non-current liabilities			
Bank loan			500
Net assets			**1800**
Equity & reserves			
Shares		1500	
Profit for the year		300	**1800**

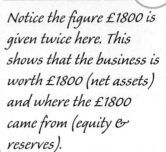

Hints & tips

Notice the figure £1800 is given twice here. This shows that the business is worth £1800 (net assets) and where the £1800 came from (equity & reserves).

Case study 5.3

Debbie's Deli

You have been given the following financial statement from Debbie's Deli. Study the information and attempt the Discussion points below.

Statement of financial position for Debbie's Deli PLC as at 31 Dec year 3			
	£000	£000	£000
Non-current assets			
Premises			800
Vehicles			200
Fixtures & fittings			100
			1100
Add **Current assets**			
Closing inventory	50		
Cash	400	450	
Less **Current liabilities**			
Bank overdraft	250		
Trade payables	150	400	
Working equity			50
Net assets			1150
Equity & reserves			
Shares		?	
Profit for the year		150	1150

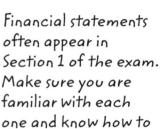

Remember

Financial statements often appear in Section 1 of the exam. Make sure you are familiar with each one and know how to **interpret** them.

Discussion points

In pairs, groups or on your own:

1 Suggest reasons for such a low working equity figure.
2 Describe the effect a low working equity figure has on net assets.
3 State the missing shares figure.
4 What would happen to the following if trade payables increased by £100 and everything else remained constant?
    a) Current assets
    b) Working equity
    c) Net assets.

Quick questions 5.3

1 **a)** Identify two users of financial information.
   b) Describe the use the users you identified in 1a) above will have for the information.
2 Define the two types of profit shown in an income statement.
3 Suggest three features of a statement of financial position.
4 Describe the term 'working equity'.
5 Outline the steps to calculate profit for the year.

Key question 5.2

Describe the purpose of two financial statements.

Activity 5.1

Practising preparing financial statements, while not required to pass the Higher Business Management course, is a good way to understand them, so you can develop skills in how to interpret them.

1 Using a spreadsheet package, such as Microsoft Excel, enter the following information to create an **Income Statement** and a **Statement of Financial Position**.
2 The figures that you need are in the table below. You aren't required to calculate them; however, it will help you understand the benefits of using a spreadsheet package if you try to enter formula to calculate them for you. Ask your teacher for help with this.
3 Use the examples in this chapter to help you enter each figure and term correctly.

	£		£
Sales revenue	4725	Profit for the year	3000
Opening inventory	225	Non-current assets	3500
Purchases	725	Cash	975
Closing inventory	300	Bank overdraft	325
Cost of sales	**650**	Trade payables	450
Gross profit	**4075**	**Working equity**	**500**
Rent	500	**Net assets**	**4000**
Wages	575	Share capital	1000

Ratio analysis

Users of financial statements, such as managers, use a number of ratios to analyse the information they provide.

Purpose of ratio analysis

- Compare the performance of the business with previous years
- Compare the performance of a business to that of its competitors
- Compare against industry averages
- Highlight areas of the business that need attention
- Highlight trends to aid future decision-making

Limitations of ratio analysis

- Ratio information is historical so is not relevant to the current or future position.
- Ratios do not take into account external factors, for example, recessions.
- Ratios do not take into account internal factors, for example, low staff morale.
- Ratios do not take into account product developments.
- It is difficult to find competitors of the *exact* type and size to make valid comparisons.

Profitability ratios

Profitability ratios measure how profitable a business is.

Table 5.9 Profitability ratios

Ratio	Description	How to improve percentage
Gross profit percentage Formula: $\dfrac{\text{gross profit}}{\text{sales revenue}} \times 100$	This measures the *percentage* of profit made from buying and selling. The higher the percentage, the better.	Increase sales revenue, e.g. by increasing prices. Switch to a cheaper supplier of purchases.
Profit for the year percentage Formula: $\dfrac{\text{profit for the year}}{\text{sales revenue}} \times 100$	This measures the *percentage* of profit made once expenses are deducted from gross profit. The higher the percentage, the better.	Reduce expenses, e.g. lower wage costs by making staff redundant. Increase sales revenue. Improve gross profit to have a knock-on effect.

Ratio	Description	How to improve percentage
Return on equity employed Formula: $$\frac{\textbf{profit for the year}}{\textbf{equity}} \times \textbf{100}$$	This measures the *percentage* of investment that is returned to investors such as shareholders. The higher the percentage, the better.	Attempt to increase profit for the year, e.g. by reducing expenses or improving revenue.

Hints & tips ⭐

You must use the word 'percentage' when describing profitability ratios. If you don't, you will only be describing a financial term, not a ratio!

Remember

A reduction in the ROEE could simply mean that more shares were issued, i.e. smaller slices of cake for more people!

Liquidity ratios

Liquidity ratios measure cash situation or the business and its ability to pay its short-term debts.

Table 5.10 Liquidity ratios

Ratio	Description	How to improve percentage
Current ratio Formula: $$\frac{\textbf{current assets}}{\textbf{current liabilities}}$$	Measures the ability of a business to pay back short-term debts. The result is expressed as X:1. Over 2:1 is ideal, as it proves the business has twice the current assets as current liabilities and a healthy cash flow.	If a business has less than 2:1, they must try and secure more current assets, e.g. by selling non-current assets for cash. They should also reduce current liabilities. If the result is too high, e.g. 4:1 or 5:1, they should invest some current assets.
Acid test ratio Formula: $$\frac{\textbf{(current assets} - \textbf{closing inventory)}}{\textbf{current liabilities}}$$	Measures the ability of a business to pay back short-term debts *in a crisis situation.* By removing inventory from the equation, the business can assess its cash flow without including the *least liquid* current asset. 1:1 is acceptable.	If a business has less than 1:1, it must secure more current assets, e.g. encouraging cash sales, to improve cash flow. If its current ratio is OK but acid test is too low, it indicates too much money tied up in inventory, so it could implement JIT inventory control to avoid this.

Efficiency ratios

Efficiency ratios measure how well a business uses its resources.

Table 5.11 Efficiency ratios

Ratio	Description	How to improve percentage
Rate of inventory turnover Formula: $$\frac{\textbf{cost of sales}}{\textbf{average inventory*}}$$ *opening inventory + closing inventory* / 2 The **rate of inventory** turnover ratio needs to be interpreted with care. Some products and businesses will have very high levels of inventory turnover: McDonald's or Asda will turnover their inventory many times a week never mind 9 times a year! It also depends when the inventory figures used are taken: perhaps because of seasonal demand the figures are higher or lower than normal. The general rule is that yes, a higher figure is better but this figure should only compare like-for-like, i.e. with previous years or similar competition.	Measures the amount of times a business re-stocks its inventory during the year. The result is expressed in times, e.g. 9 times would indicate a business sold all its inventory and ordered more, 9 times in the year.	Most businesses want a high figure as it indicates that products are selling well and money is not tied up in inventory. If the result is too low they should use JIT to avoid overstocking, sell off excess stock or perhaps negotiate sale or return with suppliers (see page 72).

Example 5.4

The following are extracts from the financial statements of Edgar & Gemona, a software development partnership.

The performance is interpreted by calculating the following ratios:
- gross profit percentage
- current ratio
- acid test ratio.

Remember

Memorise the ratio formulas as writing them out in the exam will earn you easy and quick marks.

Extract from income statement for Edgar & Gemona					
	Year 1			Year 2	
	£	£		£	£
Sales revenue		5000			5200
Less Cost of sales					
Opening inventory	500			300	
Add Purchases	2000			2800	
	2500			3100	
Less Closing inventory	300			200	
Cost of sales		2200			2900
Gross profit		2800			2300
Less Expenses		1500			1800
Profit for the year		1300			500

Extract from statement of financial position for Edgar & Gemona				
	Year 1		Year 2	
	£	£	£	£
Non-current assets		10 500		10 400
Add Current assets				
Closing inventory	300		200	
Cash	1300		900	
	1600		1100	
Less Current liabilities (Overdraft)	800		1000	
Working equity		800		100
Net assets		11 300		10 500
Equity & reserves				
Opening equity balance	10 000		10 000	
Profit for the year	1300	11 300	500	10 500

Ratio		Interpretation	How to improve
Gross profit percentage		Year 2 shows a falling GP percentage from Year 1. At first glance, revenue has improved; however, cost of sales has increased, leading to a lower gross profit percentage.	Increase sales revenue by increasing selling prices. Find a cheaper supplier of purchases.
Change for Year 1	Change for Year 2		
GP / Revenue × 100	GP / Revenue × 100		
= 2800/5000 × 100	= 2300/5200 × 100		
= 56%	= 44%		
Current ratio		Year 2 shows a falling current ratio. In Year 1 the business has an acceptable result of 2:1. In Year 2 they just cover their current liabilities with their current assets.	Increase the amount of current assets in the business, e.g. cash. Lower the amount of current liabilities in the business, e.g. pay off the overdraft.
Year 1	Year 2		
CA / CL	CA / CL		
= 1600/800	= 1100/1000		
= 2	= 1.1		
= 2:1	= 1.1:1		
Acid test ratio		Year 2 shows a falling acid test ratio. In Year 1 the business has a very acceptable result of 1.63:1. In Year 2 a result of 0.9:1 suggests that it is not able to pay off short-term debts in a crisis.	Ensure inventory isn't relied on to boost current assets by using JIT. Increase the amount of current assets in the business, e.g. cash.
Year 1	Year 2		
(CA-CI) / CL	(CA-CI) / CL		
= 1600 − 300/CL	= 1100 − 200/CL		
= 1300/800	= 900/1000		
= 1.63	= 0.9		
= 1.63:1	= 0.9:1		

Case study 5.4

Angus Ltd

The Accounting Department of Angus Ltd has provided you with ratio analysis results.

Study the information and attempt the discussion points below.

Ratio	Angus Ltd	Competitor
Gross profit ratio	45%	68%
Current ratio	5:1	2.5:1
Acid test ratio	0.95:1	1.4:1
Rate of inventory turnover	3 times	6 times
Return on equity employed	25%	20%

Discussion points

In pairs, groups or on your own:

1 Identify three areas where the competition is performing better than Angus Ltd.
2 Suggest ways for Angus Ltd to improve the areas identified in the previous question.
3 Identify one area where Angus Ltd is performing better than the competition.
4 Explain the reason for Angus Ltd's current ratio figure being so high.

Hints & tips

*You **do not** need to calculate ratios; however, understanding how they are calculated will help you to **interpret** them, which you **do** need to do successfully.*

Key questions 5.3

1 **Describe** a ratio for each of the following categories:
   a) Liquidity
   b) Profitability
   c) Efficiency
2 **Describe** two uses and two limitations of ratio analysis.

Use of technology in managing finance

Here is a summary of how technology can be used in the finance department.

- Spreadsheets can be used to prepare financial statements. This allows:
  - greater accuracy using formula, reducing the margin for error
  - formula can be replicated, saving time
  - 'What if?' statements can be used to forecast the outcome of different scenarios
  - charts and graphs can be made easily, allowing the information to be analysed and presented.
- Presentation software can be used to engage audiences when presenting information through the use of animations and colour.
- Email can be used to circulate financial information quickly.
- Local area networks (LAN) can be used to share documents so that different employees can assess and share information.
- Internet banking can be used to make payments or check balances quickly.
- Accounting software and apps such as Sage and Quickbooks can be used to keep track of payments and income and to send invoices to customers.
- EFTPOS (Electronic Funds Transfer Point Of Sale) can be used to receive money from customers instantly, e.g. through contactless payment or Apple Pay. This reduces the need for handling cash.

Remember

There are negative impacts to using any technology too; look out for examples throughout this book.

Activity 5.2

Now that we have covered all the functional areas, you may have noticed that there is some crossover when it comes to the technology used.

A useful revision activity is to look at the main software and technology, and summarise how it is used in each function.

	Technology					
	Spreadsheet	Word processing	Databases	Email	Video-conferencing	Internet
Human Resources						
Finance						
Marketing						
Operations						

1 Copy the above table, either on paper or using a word-processing package.
2 Try and write down a use of each piece of technology, specific for each functional department.
3 Ask your teacher or lecturer to check your work, but don't worry if you can't get all uses for all functions; we haven't covered all possibilities in this book.

Quick questions 5.4 ?

1 Suggest two ratios that could be calculated from the information in case study 5.1.
2 State the formula for the acid test ratio.
3 Define the following:
   a) Liquidity ratios
   b) Efficiency ratios
4 a) Identify a ratio that could be used by potential investors.
   b) State the formula for the ratio identified in a) above.
5 Justify the use of EFTPOS to complete a transaction.

Exam-style questions practice – Chapter 5

1 Justify three sources of finance for a PLC aiming to take over a competitor. **(3 marks)**
2 Explain factors affecting the source of finance chosen by an organisation. **(3 marks)**
3 Distinguish between the following:
   a) Debentures and shares
   b) Current ratio and acid test ratio. **(4 marks)**
4 Explain the ways a business can solve cash flow problems. **(5 marks)**
5 Describe the role of a manager in the finance department. **(5 marks)**
6 Describe financial statements a business can use to assess its performance. **(4 marks)**
7 Describe the limitations of ratio analysis, apart from information being historical. **(3 marks)**
8 Explain the actions required by ESQ Ltd to improve each figure in order to be more competitive. **(4 marks)**
9 Describe the term 'net assets' as seen in a Statement of Financial Position. **(3 marks)**
10 Justify the use of accounting software, such as Sage. **(4 marks)**

Exam-style case study: ASOS

Read ALL the following information and attempt ALL the questions that follow.

Internet sensation

The e-commerce company was founded almost 20 years ago as As Seen On Screen and made a name for itself selling clothes worn by celebrities, before eventually changing its name to ASOS when it began selling more items.

The firm is a hit with teens and twentysomethings thanks to its next-day delivery, vast choice and ability to quickly replenish inventory to reflect the latest trends.

The actual ASOS website itself is almost as popular as the products it sells and offers a fantastic browsing and shopping experience. ASOS constantly revises the customer browsing and ordering process, which has led to an increase in customers proceeding to the checkout and finalising their purchase. ASOS is also becoming well known for its 'A list' loyalty card. Members receive free next-day delivery and discounts. ASOS has also introduced a feature for members that guesses the best size of garment to order, based on previous orders and customer feedback on the fit.

New markets

ASOS is now planning an onslaught on the beauty market that will eat into the market share of Superdrug, Boots and the department stores. The online fashion success story, which has already taken millions of pounds in sales from high street names such as Next and Topshop, is preparing to launch its own make-up and skincare ranges. The business has also signed exclusivity deals with a number of coveted luxury skincare and make-up brands, which will see it solely stock their products on its website, and has launched its own low-cost make-up line to rival the likes of Rimmel and L'Oréal. Alex Scolding, head of buying for ASOS Face and Body, said: 'There is a big wide space in the UK beauty market between what is the mainstream and what we offer. Our customer doesn't just shop in stores, she consults YouTube, she looks at trends on social media and Pinterest. She looks at influencers to make her purchase. We aim to be that brand.'

High profits – Revenues could improve

In theory, the company's trump card in the battle with traditional retailers is the fact that – with no bricks and mortar stores to pay for – ASOS can keep its costs lower and enjoy higher profits when revenues rise and online sales increasingly dominate, as is expected in the coming years.

And, as Exhibit 1 shows, its profit margins are much higher than those of companies like Next, which are lumbered with large store estates; its gross profit is even higher than Zalando, its larger European online rival. But it is far from the best among fast-growing retailers – specialists like Superdry and JD Sports both enjoy higher gross margins, as does Boohoo.com, which is a more direct rival to ASOS.

And while its day-to-day costs are fairly low, that rapid sales growth needs lots of investment. New businesses like ASOS, Boohoo and Zalando all have much lower profit margins than the traditional stores; overtaking them in terms of popularity might be a current trend, perhaps even a fad, as there is still a long way to go to truly catch up.

Expansion

ASOS is a large business with offices in the UK as well as in Sydney, New York, Paris and Berlin. As well as offices in these locations, staff are split into specialist areas such as buying, production, finance, people and customer care. This accounts for almost 2000 employees. However, ASOS is planning on adding 1500 new roles over the next three years as well as doubling its UK manufacturing capabilities.

Following the devaluation of the pound post-Brexit, Chief Executive Officer at ASOS, Nick Beighton, has his sights set on opening a number of manufacturing plants across the UK. At the moment, ASOS produces approximately 4 per cent of its items at two factories in London. The fashion retailer sources the rest of its in-house label items from factories around the globe, including India, Turkey, China and Eastern Europe, which account for 84 per cent of all its production.

However, following the pound's decline, foreign production has become expensive and domestic production has become more affordable for retailers such as ASOS, and would see them offer a more efficient supply chain and be more responsive to changes in the market. 'There is manufacturing capacity in the UK but the skills aren't quite as available as they once were,' said Beighton.

Although the fashion retailer does teach employees how to stitch and create garments at an academy in one of its London factories, Beighton is aware of the lack of skills needed to bring more of its production to the UK. However, as the majority of ASOS sales are from outside the UK, the pound's decline has helped the fast-fashion retailer remain ahead of rivals. By cutting prices and by moving more of its sourcing to the UK, it will be able to serve its European customers faster.

Exhibit 1 – ASOS and rivals' sales revenue

— ASOS
— Next
— M&S (clothing and home)
Sales revenue (£bn)
0
1
2
3
4
5
2012
2013
2014
2015
2016
2017

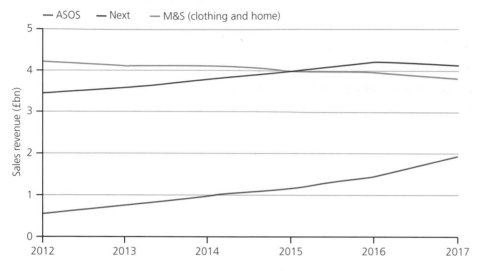

Exhibit 2 – Employee comments on Employer review site **www.glassdoor.com**

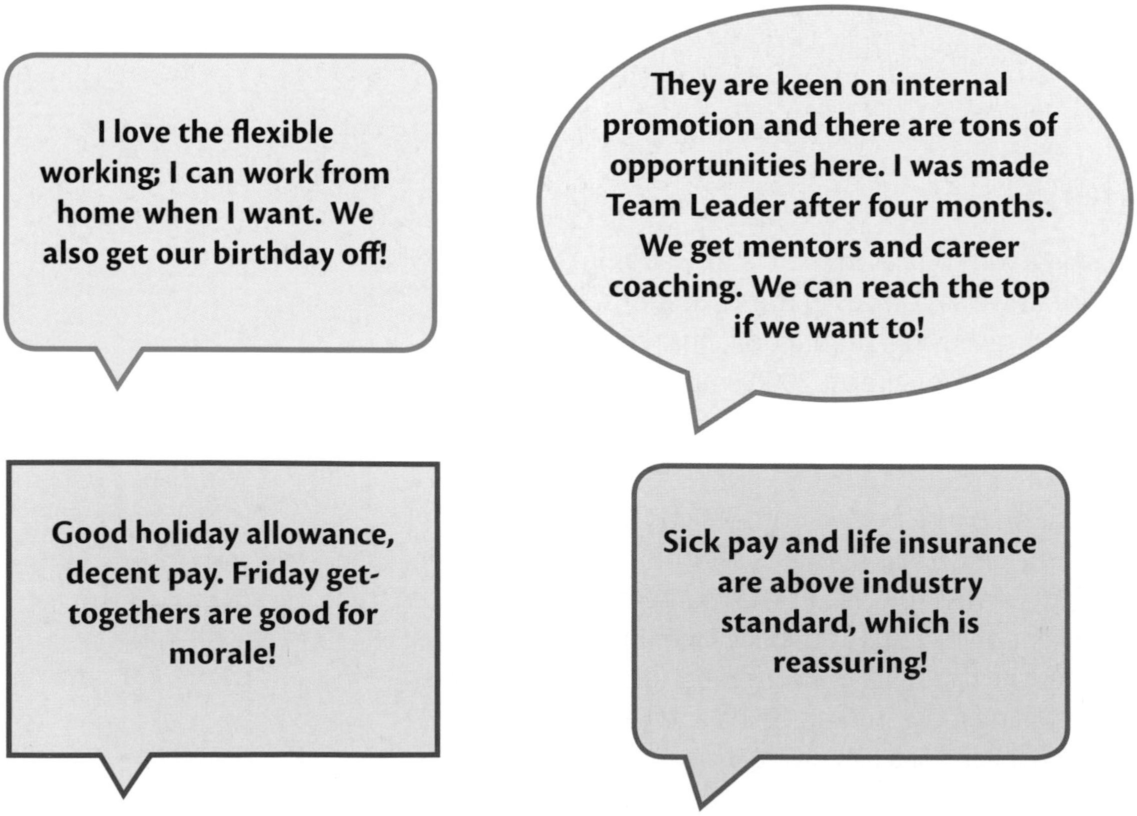

I love the flexible working; I can work from home when I want. We also get our birthday off!
They are keen on internal promotion and there are tons of opportunities here. I was made Team Leader after four months. We get mentors and career coaching. We can reach the top if we want to!
Good holiday allowance, decent pay. Friday get-togethers are good for morale!
Sick pay and life insurance are above industry standard, which is reassuring!

Exhibit 3 – The ASOS checkout experience

Features of the ASOS checkout process
● Image of item on summary
● Size, price and quantity are very clear
● Promotions such as free delivery are visible at checkout
● Free delivery
● Secure shopping
● Wide variety of payment options
● Shopping bag visible on 'mini screen' during browsing

The following questions are based on ALL the information provided and on knowledge and understanding acquired while studying the course.

1 a) Discuss the costs and benefits of the type of retailing used by ASOS.   4

   b) Using the case study, explain the use of the following elements of ASOS's marketing mix: 6
      ● Process
      ● Product
      ● Promotion

   c) i) Explain possible reasons for the trends shown in Exhibit 1.   2
      ii) Describe the financial statement that would show the figures in Exhibit 1.   3

   d) Discuss the methods of grouping used by ASOS.   6

   e) ASOS is a market-led organisation. Distinguish between market-led and product-led organisations.   2

   f) Describe, using Exhibit 2, how ASOS meets the needs of employees according to Maslow's hierarchy of needs.   5

   g) Using evidence from the case study, justify ASOS's decision to manufacture in the UK.   2

Answers and solutions

Quick questions 1.1

1   Private sector: Business owned by private individuals

    Public sector: Organisations owned by the government

    Third sector: Organisations that aim to help others

2   Primary sector: Raw materials are extracted from their natural environment

    Secondary sector: Raw materials are turned into goods

Tertiary sector: Services provided to consumers, such as selling goods

Quaternary sector: This consists of providing information and knowledge-based services, such as R&D

3   This means to increase the value of the product compared to how much it was bought from the supplier for, for example selling bread for £1.50 after the ingredients were bought for 50p.

Quick questions 1.2

1   Owned by shareholders

    Shares can be sold publicly on the stock market

    Shareholders have limited liability, i.e. they can only lose their investment and not personal possessions to creditors

2   Charities exist to raise money to help others for example Cancer Research

    Social enterprises are businesses that aim to maximise profits to help a particular cause, e.g. the Big Issue

3   Language barriers

    Time zones

    Culture differences

4   A franchise is a business model that allows businesses to pay a sum of money to own a branch of a well-known, existing business.

5   Owned by the government

    Funded through taxation

Key question 1.1

A PLC is owned by shareholders whereas a public sector organisation is owned by the government.

A PLC is financed through selling shares on the stock market whereas a public sector organisation is financed through taxes collected from the general public.

Quick questions 1.3

1   CSR (Corporate Social Responsibility) refers to organisations aiming to act in any way that benefits either society or the environment.

2   Avoiding child labour

    Recycling

    Donating to charity

3   Sector of economy, e.g. public sector won't aim to maximise profits.

    Changing circumstances, e.g. a strong competitor might force a business to satisfice for a while.

Quick questions 1.4

1 Businesses will be able to take advantage of economies of scale, such as bulk buying.

Businesses will be able to spread risk over more products/outlets, etc.

2 Demerger

Divestment

Outsourcing

3 Deintegration occurs when a business sells off part of the supply chain that it is vertically integrated with.

4 Can adversely affect core activities

New business may be inefficiently managed causing costs to rise.

Quick questions 1.5

1 Income tax, VAT and corporation tax

2 Fiscal policy is the government controlling spending through tax changes and public spending on infrastructure and large projects. Monetary policy is the government controlling the supply of money by changing interest rates.

3 Social: the UK's ageing population has seen a growth in elderly markets. There has been a rise in women taking up professional careers and managerial positions.

Technological: Cloud computing has enabled organisations to store and access information remotely. Social networking has enabled organisations to keep constant communication with customers on sites like Facebook.

4 Positive: Competition could open up a store next to a business which brings more passing trade to the area.

Quick questions 1.6

1 Managers can impact on an organisation by the level of risk they are willing to take or by the experience they have.

Employees can impact on an organisation through the level of training they have had and the levels of motivation they have to do a good job.

5 A buy-out is when existing management take over the ownership; a buy-in is when a competitor's management team takes over the business.

Key questions 1.2

1 Maximise profits

Corporate social responsibility

2 A PLC would want to maximise profits so it has as much money as possible to pay shareholders' dividends and invest in the business.

A PLC would want to have CSR aims so it can build a good reputation among society and gain more customers.

Negative: Competition could offer lower prices or better-quality products.

5 Boom – High sales

Recession – Low sales

Recovery – Sales begin to rise

Key question 1.3

Political factors could impact on a large organisation. The government could increase the minimum wage. This would mean the organisation had to pay more wages which would result in a smaller profit.

Economic factors could impact on a large organisation. The economy could be in a recession. This would mean there is high unemployment which results in customers having less money to spend in the organisation, reducing sales.

2 A business will not be able to perform to its best if it isn't fully staffed, for example producing products or serving customers quickly enough.

3 Cost of replacing and repairing technology

Breakdowns, for example losing Wi-Fi, can result in no productivity.

⇨

4 Corporate culture is the set of values, beliefs and customs that is shared by all people in an organisation.

5 Company values, e.g. a commitment to recycling or fair trade

Corporate colours, e.g. easyJet's orange or Coca-Cola's red

Open and relaxed office layout, e.g. Google

Quick questions 1.7

1 A stakeholder is an individual or group of people who have an interest in the success of an organisation.

2 Two stakeholder groups can't both get what they want.

3 The interests of HMRC are to ensure the correct amount of tax has been paid by a business.

4 Customers can decide to not buy from the business and go to the competition.

Quick questions 1.8

1 The chain of command is the flow of information and decisions through an organisation.

2 A tall management structure has many levels of management whereas a flat management structure has few levels of management.

3 a) Delayering involves removing a management level to make the structure flatter with a shorter chain of command.

b) Downsizing involves closing an unprofitable division, such as a poorly performing local branch.

4 Managers have more time for supervision, planning and decision-making.

Managers are more able to support subordinates.

5 This involves grouping an organisation into departments based on skills and expertise, e.g. marketing, finance.

Key question 1.4

Employees could affect the organisation by not being motivated, which means the standard of their work might drop, or they may provide poor customer service, which could lead to customer complaints.

The finance available could affect the organisation as, if there is no money, it will not be able to carry out decisions and courses of action it wishes to, such as expanding the business.

5 Owners need governments to make good decisions, such as lowering taxes to improve the spending power of customers while governments need owners to create jobs in the community.

Key question 1.5

Employees want a pay rise whereas owners want to keep wages low to maximise profits.

Customers want low prices and value for money whereas owners want to raise prices to maximise profits.

Key questions 1.6

1 An organisation could use functional groupings. This is when common areas of expertise and skills are grouped together, such as a marketing department, a finance department, etc.

An organisation could use an entrepreneurial management structure. This is when the business has very few key decision-makers at the core of the organisation, usually only the owner.

2 An organisation would use a functional grouping as everyone is clear about their roles and responsibilities, giving the organisation a clear structure, and staff know who to turn to for advice.

A business could use an entrepreneurial structure as it has few decision-makers so decisions can be made quickly.

Quick questions 1.9

1 A tactical decision is one made by middle managers to achieve a strategic objective, e.g. deciding on what new products to sell.
2 Comparing sales and profits

   Interviewing staff

   Reading customer review sites/social media comments

Quick questions 2.1

1 a) How consumers purchase products, e.g. using a debit card

   Where consumers purchase products, e.g. using e-commerce
  b) Need to promote products through point of sale merchandising and sales promotions

Quick questions 2.2

1 Random sampling – choosing to survey anyone at random from an extensive list

   Quota sampling – selecting respondents based on characteristics
2 Reactions to price changes can influence future pricing.

   Money-off rewards can lower profits.
3 Online

   Post

   Telephone
4 A hall test involves giving customers a sample of a product to try so that initial feedback can be observed.

Quick questions 2.3

1 The brand name of the product can be changed.

   New variations can be launched.

   The price could be lowered.
2 a) Market share – a product's percentage of sales in the market

3 SWOT allows a business to analyse its internal (*inside* the organisation) strengths and weaknesses, as well as external (*outside* the organisation) opportunities and threats.
4 Fierce competition

   Changing legislation

   Changing tastes and fashions
5 Decision-making is kept at the senior level of the business.

   Need to provide payment services, e.g. contactless payment/e-commerce facilities
2 This is when customers buy something that they didn't set out to buy; it just 'caught their eye'.
3 Products are provided based on identified consumer wants.

   High levels of market research are carried out.

5 Participants have to be paid.

   Strong personalities can influence the group's opinion.

Key question 2.1

Test marketing allows a product to be trialled in one area, which means the product can be adapted if necessary to allow a successful national launch.

Telephone surveys can be used to target specific area codes, which allows the business to meet the needs of local markets.

  b) Market growth – the overall potential for sales that the market has as a whole
3 Both have high market share; however, cash cows are in low-growth markets while stars are in a high-growth market.

Quick questions 2.4

1 Adding a percentage 'mark-up' to the unit cost of the product
2 Penetration
3 Target market

   Demand for the product

Quick questions 2.5

1 Catalogues allow customers to browse through products at home and order online or via telephone.

   Personal selling involves salespeople contacting customers directly to try and sell products.
2 Infrastructure (roads, free car parks, etc.) makes it easy for customers to get to.

   They are often near amenities such as restaurants and cinemas.

Quick questions 2.6

1 Sale or return involves products being sent back to the supplier at no cost if they can't be sold. Favourable credit terms allow businesses to pay for goods at a later date.
2 Customers might buy the product if they like it.
3 Press conferences involve the media being invited to a business presentation to be given information or news.
   The business could sponsor a team or event.
   The business could donate to charity.

Quick questions 2.7

1 Staff are well trained.
   Staff are monitored and checked to ensure they are providing excellent customer service.
   Don't appoint staff 'on a whim'.
2 Self-scan checkouts
   Contactless payment/Apple Pay
3 Colour schemes, fonts and images used should appeal to the target market.

Key questions 2.2

1 The price could be decreased. This would mean the product is more affordable to more market segments and so increase sales.
   The business could sell online using e-commerce. This would mean a worldwide market could be reached.

4 Charging different prices for different types of customer, e.g. different ages
5 Higher prices are charged initially due to the hype of a new product.

   Lack of competition also allows maximum prices to be charged.

   Larger store sizes mean a good product range can be stocked.
3 High prices are charged due to high overheads.

   It is less convenient than online shopping.
4 Retailers are located close the customers, e.g. in towns, shopping centres.
5 A wholesaler buys goods in bulk from manufacturers and then sells them on to retailers.

4 Disadvantage: The business could face difficult questions and make the situation worse.
   Advantage: The business can have a chance to respond to negative publicity and give confidence back to consumers.
5 a) Celebrity endorsement involves the use of celebrities to promote the product.
   b) Product placement involves products appearing in films, TV or video games.

2 Advantages:
   - A business can use newer products to replace those at the end of the product life cycle.
   - Cash cows (high market share/low market growth) can be used to fund riskier ventures such as promoting stars (high market share/ high market growth) products to keep them ahead of the competition.

   Disadvantages:
   - Costs are high to research and develop a variety of products.
   - Dogs (low market share/low market growth) can drain a business's profits unless they are sold off.

Quick questions 2.8

1 Social media posts/feedback

   Emails can be sent to inform and ask for feedback.

   EPOS can work alongside loyalty schemes to collect information and allow promotions to be targeted.

2 Digital screens use moving images so are more likely to capture attention.

   Digital screens can play multiple adverts rather than showing just one poster.

3 Can be used to access the internet to purchase products through m-commerce.

Quick questions 3.1

1 Avoids running out of inventory and then placing an order without having a 'buffer'.

2 The process of ordering supplies only when they are required.

3 Databases keep balances of inventory which are automatically updated.

   Can be linked to tills through EPOS, which updates inventory levels with each sale.

4 Inventory

   Storage

   Distribution

5 Labels should include maximum, minimum, and re-order level. The x axis should be labelled 'Time' and the y axis should be labelled 'Inventory level'. Lead time and buffer inventory should also be annotated for full marks.

Quick questions 3.2

1 Products are produced in exactly the same way every time, improving consistency.

   Fewer mistakes are made, which limits waste.

2 Advantage – Humans can use initiative and creativity, which is often lacking in automated systems.

   Disadvantage – Humans have to take breaks, holidays, etc., which limits production time.

3 Employees become efficient at their role by repeating the same tasks routinely.

Can be used to purchase apps for businesses to target promotions and services to.

Can be used to access social media, which businesses can use to promote products on.

Key question 2.3

The internet can be used to advertise products, targeted to customer wants through browsing histories.

Self-checkout systems can be used to speed up the process of purchasing products.

6 Inventory should be on ground level only.

   Large loading bay with easy access

   Technology utilised to improve speed and accuracy, e.g. barcode scanning, robotics

Key questions 3.1

1 Maximum inventory level – the most amount of inventory a business should hold.

   Minimum inventory level – the least amount of inventory a business should hold.

2 So the business doesn't overstock, which means there is less chance of inventory going out of date.

   So the business doesn't understock, which means they cannot satisfy demand, resulting in customers going elsewhere.

Key questions 3.2

1 Job production – This involves making unique one-off products to a customer's specifications.

   Batch production – This is when groups of similar products are made at a time.

2 **Job production**

   Advantage – Produces a unique, high-quality product which means high prices can be charged.

   Disadvantage – The high skill of staff will mean high wages will need to be paid.

Batch production

Advantage – Can allow for changes to products to be made easily as all the machinery is standardised.

Quick questions 3.3

1 Poor-quality goods can result in customers returning their purchase, which results in lost sales.

 High-quality goods can result in a good reputation and new customers buying from the business.

2 Everyone in the organisation focuses on quality.

 Results in zero errors.

3 Benchmarking involves copying the quality of a finished product, and the processes used to achieve it, as used by the market leader.

4 No bias is shown as the mystery shopper isn't employed by the business.

 Valuable feedback is given regarding whether or not the customer experience is satisfactory.

5 BSI Kitemark

 CE Mark

 Industry stars – e.g. Hotels, Euro NCAP

Quick questions 3.4

1 Advantage – fair trade products can appeal to customers who appreciate the ethics of the product.

 Disadvantage – fair trade products are more expensive than non-Fairtrade certified products and there is less choice.

2 Using alternative sources of 'renewable' energy, such as solar and wind

 Using low emissions vehicles or EVs

Quick questions 4.1

1 New staff may be needed, for example due to increasing demand for existing products.

 Existing staff may have to be removed due to retirement, maternity leave, etc.

2 Analyse demand

 Analyse skills of current staff

 'Close the gaps', e.g. train or hire

3 The vacancy can be filled quickly.

Disadvantage – Staff and machinery may be idle between batches, increasing costs.

Key questions 3.3

1 Quality control involves inspecting finished goods and raw materials.

 Quality standards involves a product being awarded a symbol for meeting an agreed standard.

2 Quality control:
 ● No unsatisfactory products are sold to customers, which means no products are returned.
 ● The business does not end up with a bad reputation, as no faulty products are sold.

 Quality standards:
 ● A symbol awarded for meeting standards can be used for marketing purposes, which can attract customers.
 ● A higher price can be charged as the product is proven to be of high quality.

3 Reusable packaging

 Recyclable packaging

 Biodegradable packaging

Key question 3.4

CAM (computer aided manufacture) uses robotics to completely automate the production process.

Computerised inventory (stock) management systems can automatically re-order inventory.

 The organisation will know the traits/skills of the candidate.

4 These involve an applicant being employed for a short while to make sure they are capable of doing the job and are reliable.

5 A large number of applicants are seen at the same time.

 Applicants are scrutinised through team-building/role-play exercises/tests, etc.

Quick questions 4.2

1 Apprentices actually contribute while training.

   Apprentices are paid which can be motivational.

2 Graduates can be moulded with the skills and knowledge desired by the business.

3 Can develop their skills

   Can command higher wages/promotions

4 A 360-degree appraisal involves the peer or line manager, who conducts the appraisal, giving feedback from fellow employees, supervisors and subordinates.

5 Training courses

   Professional reading

Quick questions 4.3

1 Performance related pay/commission

   Development opportunities

   Empowerment

2 There are two sets of factors: motivators which motivate staff if present and hygiene factors which demotivate staff if missing, e.g. basic clean working conditions.

3 Safety and security – Staff need a contract of employment to give them job security.

   Self-esteem – Staff are motivated by having an important job title and recognition of their achievements in front of peers.

Quick questions 4.4

1 Negative public image

   Redundancy payments can be expensive.

2 Before dismissal, employers must be able to give account of the policies the employee has broken and the procedures and sanctions that have been used.

   Employers should use a fair and consistent procedure when dismissing employees.

3 a) ACAS is a government-funded organisation that attempts to solve disputes in the workplace to stop them going to court.

   b) A trade union is an organisation that represents a group of employees. Employees benefit from standing together

Key question 4.1

Human resources (HR) could use workforce planning to ensure that the organisation has the number of staff, with the correct skills, to meet the needs of the organisation at the time they are required.

HR could use methods of testing, such as aptitude tests, to ensure applicants for new positions have the required skills and abilities to work effectively in the organisation, e.g. giving an accountant a numerical test.

4 Poorer productivity/service

   High staff absenteeism

   High staff turnover

5 Managers let employees have a say in decision-making.

Key question 4.2

Setting up a works council/consultative committee, where an equal number of employees and managers have joint decision-making powers.

Paying employees a 'piece rate', which is paying per item produced and encourages a high work rate.

(collective bargaining), the experience of the union leaders and the legal powers the union has.

4 A grievance is a concern, problem or complaint raised by an employee, for example, to do with working conditions, relationships with colleagues, or a complaint about their manager.

5 Worker director

   Works council

   Quality circles

Key question 4.3

Maintaining good employee relations by consulting with employees on any major

⇨

changes that are about to take place, especially if it will impact on their working day, such as a new office layout or new procedures, will reduce the chances of employees resisting change.

Quick questions 4.5

1 Saves travel costs and time.
   Can see facial reactions/appearance so better than telephone interview.
2 Some employees prefer face-to-face contact. Difficult to supervise training.
3 Age, disability, gender
4 Harassment – Behaviour that is deemed offensive by the recipient due to a protected characteristic.

   Direct discrimination – Someone is treated less favourably than another person because of a protected characteristic.
5 The living wage is the minimum pay per hour most workers over 25 are entitled to. The minimum wage is the minimum for under 25s.

Quick questions 5.1

1 Expensive equipment can be bought with only an initial deposit and manageable monthly instalments.
2 Small amounts of money from a large number of people are raised to fund a new business or a project, e.g. Kickstarter.
3 Advantage – Guaranteed to get some money back

   Disadvantage – Have to sell the debt to the factoring firm for less than it is worth
4 UK Government

   The Prince's Trust
5 Trade credit

   Overdraft

Quick questions 5.2

1 To allow investment ahead of surpluses

   To allow for solutions to be found ahead of deficits

Negative employee relations can result in industrial action, such as a strike whereby employees refuse to work, which will result in no work being done, no goods being made or sold and customers going to the competition.

6 Take care of their own safety.

   Report any incidents.
7 The business can be fined.

   The business will have a poor public image.

Key questions 4.4

1 National Minimum Wage Act 1998.
2 The National Minimum Wage Act 1998 makes it illegal to pay an employee below a certain amount per hour as long as employees meet the age criteria to qualify for each minimum rate. Any increase to the minimum wage by the government will increase the costs to the business and so lower profits.

Key questions 5.1

1 A loan from a bank is paid back with interest added.

   Shares could be sold which are small fragments of ownership sold either privately or on the stock market.
2 A bank loan is paid back in manageable monthly instalments, which makes it easier to pay back and to budget for.

   Huge amounts of finance can be raised selling shares on the stock market, which can be used to grow the business, for example, to open new stores.

2 Discounts for paying in cash

   High interest rates for paying with credit
3 Wages, rent, asset purchases (e.g. van)

Quick questions 5.3

1 a) Owners

   Employees

   b) Owners – To assess profit levels/make decisions

   Employees – To check profits to ensure jobs are secure

2 It shows the gross profit, which is the profit made from buying and selling inventory.

   It shows the PFTY (profit for the year), which is the profit after expenses have been deducted from gross profit.

3 It shows the non-current assets.

   It shows the current assets.

   It shows the current liabilities.

Quick questions 5.4

1 Gross profit percentage

   Profit for the year percentage

2 $\dfrac{(\text{current assets} - \text{closing inventory})}{\text{current liabilities}}$

3 a) Liquidity ratios measure the ability of the business to pay its debts.

   b) Efficiency ratios measure how well a business uses its resources.

4 a) ROEE (return on equity employed)

   b) $\dfrac{\text{PFTY} \times 100}{\text{equity}}$

5 Can speed up transactions and reduce the need for cash handling.

4 Working equity is current assets – current liabilities. This shows how easily a business can pay its short-term debts.

5 Sales revenue – cost of sales – expenses

Key question 5.2

An income statement calculates the profitability of the business by working out the Gross profit which is the profit made from buying and selling, and the overall profit for the year which is the profit once expenses are deducted from gross profit.

A statement of financial position calculates the value and worth of an organisation at a specific point in time. It shows what the organisation's assets and liabilities are.

Key questions 5.3

1 a) Current ratio – CA/CL

   b) PFTY % – PFTY/SR x 100

   c) ROIT – COS/AI

2 Uses:

   ● To compare with previous years/competitors

   Limitations:

   ● Ratio information is historical

   ● No consideration of external factors is taken

Solutions to exam-style questions

Example

Exam-style solutions

Set 1

1 A PLC can sell shares to anyone through the stock market **whereas** a Ltd company can only sell shares to private individuals they know such as employees.

   Both a PLC and a Ltd company have limited liability, which is when owners (shareholders) are only at risk of losing their investment and not personal possessions.

   Both a PLC and a Ltd company are controlled by a board of directors.

2 Social enterprises:
   - can attract customers who appreciate their social cause
   - can also attract good-quality staff who want to work for an organisation that makes a difference
   - are likely to receive help from the government, e.g. grants, because they impact on society
   - benefit from an asset lock so the sale of assets, if they go bust, go to their good cause.

3 Advantages
   - Franchiser is able to grow with minimal risk.
   - Franchiser receives a share of the profits.

   Disadvantages
   - If one individual franchise gets a bad reputation it will affect the whole brand.
   - The franchiser misses out on all the profits if they grew organically.

4 A multinational organisation:
   - has operations in more than one country
   - usually bases its head office in its home country
   - can influence governments and receive grants for creating jobs.

5 To grow organically, a business could:
   - launch new products/services **which means** businesses can meet the needs of different market segments
   - open new physical branches by opening up in new locations **meaning** they can reach new markets and more customers
   - introduce e-commerce, selling online **which means** the business can trade 24/7 around the world ⇨

Hints & tips

*Remember, when the command word 'compare' is used, to write **whereas** to make a point of distinction (differences) between two related factors and **both** to make a point of similarity between two related factors.*

Hints & tips

*Remember when asked to 'explain' you must relate cause and **effect**. Here, the cause is given first and the **effect** is then explained. Show the examiner you are explaining the **effect** by writing key link phrases such as **this means, meaning, this will, so** etc. between your cause and the effect you explain.*

- expand their existing premises **which means** they can cater for more products/staff and make more sales
- could hire more staff. **This will** improve the business's ability to make more sales or develop more products.

6 Advantages:
- Outsourcing allows a business to concentrate on core activities.
- Less labour and equipment required for outsourced activities, e.g. saving on printers and reprographics staff.
- Outsourced business may provide the service cheaper than in-house as they can benefit from economies of scale.

Disadvantages:
- Communication between businesses needs to be very clear to make sure exact specifications are met.
- May have to share sensitive information .
- Outsourcing could be more expensive than in-house as specialists and expertise come at a price.

7 Merger:
A business could agree to join with another business. An advantage of this would be increased market share.

However, a disadvantage could be customers being put off the new business and leaving altogether.

Takeover:
A business could acquire another business. An advantage of this could be the acquisition of resources such as retail outlets or production facilities.

However, a disadvantage is takeovers are often hostile which could lead to a bad public image.

8 Decentralised management:
- delegates decision-making to individual departments **whereas** centralised decision-making retains decision-making at head office
- results in the organisation losing an overall corporate image if each department/branch is operating differently **whereas** with centralised a high degree of corporate identity and strategy exists as decisions are made for the whole organisation
- allows more subordinates to be empowered which encourages creativity and results in motivated staff **whereas** with centralised less responsibility is given to subordinates which can result in demotivated staff.

9 Interest rates can increase **which means** customers have less disposable income to spend on business's goods and services **due to** higher borrowing costs.

Interest rates can decrease **which means** customers are less likely to save **because of** unattractive rates and **therefore** will spend more on organisation's products

Hints & tips

*'Discuss' questions don't **need** to be explained; however, here, the point about the cost of outsourcing is being discussed as both an advantage and a disadvantage – so that must be made clear.*

Hints & tips

'Discuss' questions tend to only be awarded marks for costs and benefits, so write about costs/benefits up to the mark allocation, even if you write a brief definition too.

Hints & tips

*Only **differences** are awarded marks in 'Distinguish' questions.*

The economic cycle can affect an organisation in a positive way **as** during times of boom/recovery customers are more likely to be in a position to spend **because** employment rates are higher **meaning** sales will increase.

The economic cycle can affect an organisation in a negative way **as** during a recession unemployment is high **which** reduces disposable income. **This means** customers are less likely to be in a position to spend so sales will fall and **furthermore** the business may have to take drastic action such as downsizing.

10 Organisations:
- can't collude with other organisations to fix prices in cartels. If found guilty of participating in cartels, owners or management can be fined or even sentenced to prison.
- can have potential mergers blocked if it is likely to lower competition substantially in their market.
- can't use their dominant position in the market to charge drastically low prices, pay lower prices to suppliers or control the supply of goods.

Example

Exam-style solutions

Set 2

1   A positive corporate culture can make employees feel part of the organisation through the use of uniforms, jargon and language etc. **which will** increase motivation.

A positive corporate culture will mean a lower staff turnover **as** employees want to remain part of the organisation, **therefore** saving money on recruitment and training costs.

A business known for a positive corporate culture will attract the best staff **because** they want to be part of the organisation and experience the culture.

A culture of openness and flexible working arrangements **will mean** staff work when and where suits them best and **so** will perform better.

Through rituals such as 'dress down Friday' a relaxed environment can be created **which will** enable staff relationships to be forged **which will** encourage collaboration and increase both creativity and productivity.

2   Factors that affect quality decisions being made:
- Managers who have the ability and experience to make good decisions and are willing to take risks when making decisions.

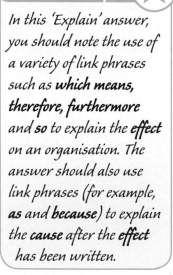

Hints & tips

In this 'Explain' answer, you should note the use of a variety of link phrases such as **which means, therefore, furthermore** and **so** to explain the **effect** on an organisation. The answer should also use link phrases (for example, **as** and **because**) to explain the **cause** after the **effect** has been written.

- Staff resistance to change can stop a decision being actioned.
- Financial constraints may mean that the organisation cannot choose the best solution to a problem.
- The quality of the information available on which to base the decision may be poor, e.g. out of date, biased, not relevant etc.

3   Benefits of the matrix structure:
- Each team has staff from all functional areas **which means** a good amount of experience as there are skills in each project team.
- Complex problems can be solved **as** they have decision-makers with good skills and experience.
- Staff can use their expertise **which means** they feel valued and are motivated.

4   Advantages:
- Each division can meet the needs of local markets **which means** customer loyalty will build up.
- The business can react to changing external (PESTEC) factors, such as competition cutting prices, as each group is close to the local market.
- Easy to identify a failing group **which means** divisional mangers can be held accountable and changes made.

Disadvantages:
- Duplication of resources, such as administration staff or IT equipment across each group **which will** increase costs to the organisation.

5   Customer grouping is arranging staff that deal with specific customer types to work together **whereas** product grouping staff that deal with specific products/service work together.
Customer grouping can tailor its service to each type of customer **whereas** product grouping can tailor its service to the target market for the product.

Through comparing group sales to each customer it is easy to see which customer group is performing poorly, **whereas** it is easy to see which product group is poorly performing through comparing sales of each product.
Both groupings duplicate resources.

6   A strategic decision is a long-term decision **whereas** an operational decision is a day-to-day decision.

A strategic decision is made by senior managers **whereas** an operational decision is made by all staff or low-level supervisors.

A strategic decision is the long-term objectives of the organisation such as 'to grow' **whereas** an operational decision is a routine task such as staff lunch rotas.

7   Advantages of using a structured decision making model, such as SWOT analysis are:

Remember

... 'duplication of resources' is a disadvantage of all groupings except Functional!

Hints & tips

Always remember to use **whereas** *here to show the points of distinction between the two factors and make sure the points are related and not just random! In this case the points of distinction are* **length of decision, decision maker** *and* **type of decision**. *Make sure your points are related!*

- it identifies strengths and allows a business to build upon them, e.g. having a good brand name so launching new products.
- it identifies weaknesses and allows them to be addressed, e.g. poorly performing branch so downsizing and closing it.
- it identifies threats and allows them to be turned into opportunities, e.g. embracing advancing technology, not allowing it to leave the business behind.

However, disadvantages are:
- a SWOT analysis is very time consuming, which can slow down decision making.
- a SWOT analysis is a very structured process, which can stifle creativity and gut reactions from managers.

8 Role of a manager:
- Plan: Looking ahead, seeing potential opportunities, or problems, setting targets and strategies.
- Command: Issue instructions, informing staff, motivating staff.
- Co-ordinate: Bringing together the resources of the business to achieve the overall objectives.
- Control: Measuring and correcting the activities in the organisation. A manager looks at what is being done and checks it against what was expected.
- Delegate: Give subordinates the authority to carry out management-level tasks. This helps lessen manager's workload motivates staff.

9 Advantages of using technology to aid decision-making:
- Spreadsheets can improve the accuracy of calculations **because** formula can perform 'What if' statements to calculate the projected outcome of a decision.
- Databases can improve the speed of decision-making **as** they make it easy to search for information quickly using queries and to sort functions.
- Email can be used to communicate information regarding decisions to many employees at once and attachments containing information can be sent **which means** printing costs are reduced.
- Video-conferencing can reduce the need for managers to travel to meetings **which** saves time and travel costs.

10 Costs of downsizing to an organisation:
- Valuable skills and knowledge will be lost **because** staff will be made redundant through branches, departments or individuals being made redundant.
- Remaining staff will feel threatened and demotivated **which means** the quality of their work may suffer.
- Redundancies will have to be made **which means** redundancy payments will have to be paid.

Hints & tips ★

Here, examples help make these points much stronger and let the examiner see that you know more than just what SWOT stands for.

Hints & tips ★

This question needs to be answered in **context**, i.e. each answer has to come back to how technology aids a manager make a decision and not just explain an advantage of technology.

Hints & tips ★

Notice the first point explains the **cause**, which is often quite obvious, and sometimes much easier than explaining the **effect**.

Exam-style questions practice – Chapter 2

Example

Exam-style solutions

1 Advantages and disadvantages of desk research:
   - Desk research is cost effective **because** information is free to gather using published materials.
   - Desk research is quick to gather **which** allows the business to spend time on other activities such as developing products.
   - However, desk research might be biased **as** it was collated by someone else.
   - Desk research may also not be appropriate to the business's needs **because** it was gathered for another purpose.

2 a) Market-led businesses develop products based on customer wants **whereas** product-led businesses produce products that they believe customers will want and try to convince them to buy them.

   Market-led businesses rely heavily on market research **whereas** product-led businesses focus more on product research and development.

   b) In quota sampling respondents are picked according to certain characteristics **whereas** with random the respondents are picked randomly.

   Quota can be biased as the interviewer will decide who to pick for the sample **whereas** random has no bias in the selection of the sample.

Hints & tips

*Notice the use of **whereas** AND the fact that comparison points are related points.*

3 Development:
   - The business actually makes a loss at this stage **as** the product isn't on sale and the costs of development and research are high. Sales are zero **because** the product hasn't been launched onto the market yet.

   Growth:
   - Profits are low **because** promotion costs are high to raise awareness of the product. Sales are being made but progress is slow **as** customers are still unsure of the new product.

   Saturation:
   - Profits begin to fall **as** the market has attracted many competition products. Sales also begin to fall although extension strategies could be used such as lowering the price **which will** encourage extra sales.

4 Activities carried out in the R & D stage:
   - Market research will be carried out to establish a viable idea.
   - Prototypes will be made.
   - Prototypes will be tested.
   - Changes will be made in line with the feedback received.
   - A launch strategy will be developed (e.g. brand name, marketing campaign etc.). ⇨

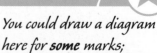

Hints & tips

*You could draw a diagram here for **some** marks; however, you will still have to explain the effect on each stage.*

5 Benefits of using a psychological pricing strategy:
- The price will be set just below a whole number **which will** make the customer think the product is much cheaper than it actually is.
- The product will be able to come into customers' search criteria or thought process **as** they may be searching for a product under a certain amount.

6 Trends in retailer types in recent years:
- There has been a trend in out-of-town retail parks that have large stores, free car parking and are close to road networks.
- There has also been a trend in convenience supermarkets, situated in convenient busy places such as city centres and train stations.
- There has been a trend in massive hypermarkets that sell many goods and services under one roof.

7 Advantages and disadvantages of a retailer using a wholesaler rather than going to the manufacturer:
- A retailer has the advantage of not having to pay for storing many items at once.
- A retailer can take advantage of promotions offered by wholesalers that manufacturers may not offer.
- **However**, a retailer will have to pay more for products.
- They may also miss out on exclusivity deals offered by manufacturers.

8 Through social media:
- Users 'like' or 'follow' the business's page so businesses can target customers or potential customers easily.
- Businesses can let customers know of new products or promotions using social media.
- Customers can leave comments allowing simple and effective market research.
- **However**, a disadvantage is customers can leave negative comments.

Using apps:
- Services can be offered for a fee, such as music downloads or products sold via m-commerce.
- Apps can have integrated activities such as games to engage users and expose them to the brand.
- A business can target 'in-app' promotions to customers based on their browsing history.

9 a) Physical evidence:
- Settings should convey the desired ambience and furnishing **so that** the customer experience is what they would have expected from the brand.
- Premises should be clean and tidy **which means** customers don't think of the business as careless and negligent.

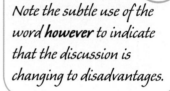

b) Process:
- Queues and waiting times should be as short as possible **to avoid** customers feeling frustrated.
- Technology such as self-checkouts and contactless payment can be introduced **resulting in** customers feeling that the point-of-sale process was swift.

10 Benefits to a business of using e-commerce:
- Customers anywhere in the world can purchase products **meaning** a worldwide customer reach.
- Online discounts can be offered **which will** attract customers away from more expensive retail outlets.
- Customers can access product information immediately, e.g. inventory availability **which means** customers save time on fruitless trips to retail outlets.
- More choice for customers online than what a high street outlet could stock and display **because** an entire range of products can be shown online.

> **Hints & tips** ★
> **Which will** helps explain the effect and **because** helps explain the cause. Either is acceptable.

Exam-style questions practice – Chapter 3

Example

Exam-style solutions

1 Re-order quantity:
- This is the amount of inventory that is ordered which will ensure the amount ordered will re-stock to the maximum level.

Minimum inventory level:
- This is the least amount of inventory that should be held which will avoid running out of inventory completely and ensure production can continue.

Buffer inventory:
- Extra inventory held to ensure there is enough to continue production if inventory levels fall below the minimum.

2 JIT inventory control:
- JIT allows for no wastage of leftover inventory.
- No money is tied up in inventory.
- Costs are saved, for example warehouse rent.
- Businesses won't be left with inventory that can't be sold, for example due to changing fashions.

3 Factors considered when setting a minimum inventory level:
- The relationships with suppliers will need to be considered **as** if they are not good a high minimum inventory level will need to be set to ensure there is a supply of materials should deliveries be late.

> **Hints & tips** ★
> Only advantages/benefits attract marks in a 'Justify' question.

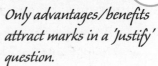

- The skill levels of staff will need to be high **because** materials can't be wasted if a very low level is set.
- The finance available will need to be considered **as** if cash flow is an issue a low minimum level will tie less money up in inventory.

4 Advantages:
- Outsourcing company will have to pay for purchasing and maintaining delivery fleet.
- Outsourcing company will be experts in matters of legislation affecting drivers.
- The business won't be at risk of rising fuel costs.
- The outsourcing company will provide an efficient logistics service.
- Outsourcing company may have greater geographical coverage allowing the organisation to reach a wider market.

5 Advantages:
- It may be cheaper to pay for one large central warehouse than many smaller warehouses.
- Large centralised warehouses can allow the business to benefit from economies of scale through bulk buying.
- They allow for the same consistent procedures to be used all over the world.
- Unlike many smaller warehouses in many different countries security against theft is tightened.

6 **a)** Capital intensive and labour intensive:
- Capital intensive involves using mostly machinery to produce goods **whereas** labour intensive is using mostly human labour to produce goods.
- Capital intensive can use CAM and robotics which can work 24/7 **whereas** labour-intensive humans need breaks and holidays so 24/7 production isn't as easy.

b) Mechanisation and automation:
- **Both** mechanisation and automation involve using machinery to produce goods.
- Mechanisation still involves labour to control the machinery **whereas** automation produces goods independent of human control.

7 Reasons for the method of production chosen by a manufacturer:
- If the workforce is highly skilled, their expertise would be better suited to labour-intensive production.
- If labour is expensive then capital intensive may work out cheaper in the long term.
- There might not be the finance to fund expensive capital such as an automated production line so labour intensive will be preferred.

8 **a)** Advantages:
- Employees are motivated by being involved in decision making.
- The business gets feedback from those actually producing the products.

Hints & tips ★

This may seem tricky but the answer is just advantages of outsourcing twisted to the context of logistics!

Hints & tips ★

Many 'Factors' questions can be answered by writing about **internal factors**, as long as they are in the context of the question. Notice how each answer above refers back to a **production method**!

Hints & tips ★

You won't get full marks by just focusing on either advantages or disadvantages — the question has asked for both!

- Employee relations are improved by staff and management working together.

Disadvantages:
- Employees meet during company time.
- Employees have to be trained to join a quality circle.

b) Other methods of ensuring quality:
- Quality control – inspecting raw materials or finished goods to check they are acceptable.
- Quality assurance – attempting to prevent poor-quality products by checking at different stages of the process.
- Continual improvement – attempting to improve every process and system.

9 Ways an operations department can achieve the ethical and environmental considerations of a positive CSR policy:
- Products should consider animal welfare such as not testing on animals. **This means** they may be awarded the 'leaping bunny' logo which can be used for marketing purposes.
- The operations department could use fair trade suppliers or stock fair trade products **which means** they will attract customers who appreciate their ethical stance.
- Renewable energies (e.g. wind energy) can be used to power factories and offices **which will** save costs in the long run.
- Operations could consider using sustainable raw materials **meaning** they ensure a future supply.
- Waste should be disposed of appropriately **which will** avoid any prosecutions and time-consuming inspections from environmental regulators.

10 By using spreadsheets in the operations department:
- Formulas can be used to accurately calculate inventory re-order quantities.
- Graphs/charts can be produced to compare inventory levels of different products.

Exam-style questions practice – Chapter 4

Example

Exam-style solutions

1 Advantages of external recruitment:
- Fresh, new ideas and skills are brought into the organisation.
- Avoids creating a further vacancy in the organisation.
- Avoids jealousy and resistance being created by one employee being promoted over others. ⇨

Disadvantages of external recruitment:
- Candidates don't know the organisation so induction training will have to be carried out.
- The organisation doesn't know the candidate which carries a risk that they may not be suited for the job, or are untrustworthy.
- Staff will be demotivated as there is no internal promotion.

2 Advantages of attainment tests:
- They allow applicants a chance to demonstrate their skills related to the post.
- Performances can be easily compared.

Disadvantages of attainment tests:
- Tests can be time consuming to carry out for managers/HR staff.
- Applicants may be put under too much pressure.
- Once hired candidates may not perform to the levels assessed in the test.

3 Steps involved in workforce planning:
- The organisation analyses the potential demand for their goods/services and decides how many staff are needed and the skills required.
- The organisation may take PESTEC factors into account.
- Staffing forecast to highlight a shortage/surplus of staff.
- The organisation analyses the profile of its current workforce to determine the need for new staff.
- The skills that require to be developed within existing staff should be analysed.
- The organisation 'closes the gaps' to ensure that it has the workforce required to provide the goods and services to meet its objectives.
- Train existing staff/recruit new staff/retain existing staff.
- The organisation will monitor and measure the impacts of the planning cycle.

4 a)
By way of corporate training schemes:
- Staff will become highly skilled.
- Staff may be candidates for promotion once trained.

b)
- Graduate training scheme – This places university graduates on an intense programme of training courses and work over a number of years.
- Apprenticeship – This allows staff to gain a formal qualification while training and working in the business.

5 Methods of appraisal:
a) 360 degree
A complete profile of the employee is gained from subordinates, peers and superiors.

Hints & tips ★

There is nothing wrong with a bulleted list like this as long as each bullet is written in a proper sentence.

Hints & tips ★

Only state advantages in a 'Justify' question.

⇨

b) Peer to peer

Employees may relax more and react better to a review given by a colleague.

6 According to Herzberg:

- Hygiene factors will not necessarily motivate employees.
- If hygiene factors are absent, however, they can lower motivation.
- Examples of hygiene factors are safe working conditions/clean staff toilets/breaks etc.
- If any one hygiene factor is missing it can be responsible for demotivating the workforce.

7 **a)**

Factors that would affect the leadership style of a manager:

- The task itself will affect the leadership style as a complex task will require more direction from management so an autocratic style would be required, while a creative task would benefit from a hands-off approach so a laissez-faire style would be suited.
- There may be less time to complete a project so a more direct autocratic style will be required.
- Highly skilled and competent staff will need less supervision, leading to democratic or laissez-faire styles being chosen.
- Poorly motivated employees can't be trusted to have the self-discipline to make their own decisions and complete tasks without instruction and supervision so autocratic leadership will be chosen.

b)

With an autocratic style control over tasks and instructions is retained by the leader **whereas** with laissez-faire control is delegated to employees who set their own tasks.

- An autocratic style can demotivate staff as there are less opportunities or delegation and empowerment **whereas** with a laissez-faire style staff are highly empowered and likely to be more motivated at work.

8 Impact of negative employee relations on an organisation:

- If employee relations are negative then employees will leave for a better work environment - increasing staff turnover **which will** mean an increase in training and recruitment/selection costs.
- Negative employee relations result in less co-operation of staff **which will** make changes harder to introduce and more likely to be unsuccessful.
- There will be an increase in grievances **which** ties up managers' time to deal with the grievances.
- In extreme cases industrial action will take place **which could** give the business a bad reputation meaning they will find it hard to recruit quality staff in the future.

⇨

9 Methods of employee participation:
- Worker directors involves a low-level employee being given a seat on the Board of Directors so employees feel that they have a voice in decision making.
- Works councils are groups made up of an equal number of employees and managers to discuss major suggestions for changes in the organisation which avoids resistance to change.
- Consultative committees involve all stakeholders, including employees to get a holistic view of decisions.

10 Disadvantages of VLE for training staff:
- The virtual learning environment can be costly because of web hosting/web design/paying for content etc.
- Lack of supervision which means there is no guarantee staff will complete all elements of training.
- Some staff prefer real face-to-face contact and will feel isolated through virtual learning.
- Breakdowns/technical problems may result in staff being unable to train.

Exam-style questions practice – Chapter 5

Example

Exam-style solutions

1 3 sources of finance for a PLC aiming to take over a competitor:
- Share issue – huge sums of money can be raised by selling shares publicly on the stock market.
- Sale of assets – can raise money without going into debt.
- Debt factoring – cash injection from the sale of trade receivables can be used to purchase the competitor.

2 Factors affecting the source of finance chosen by an organisation:
- The payback term will be considered **because** if finance can't be repaid quickly a source with a longer repayment term, e.g. a mortgage or a loan, would be chosen over shorter-term finance such as trade credit.
- The interest rates would be considered as the higher the interest the more money will have to be paid back.
- The type of organisation has to be considered: **for example** often new businesses or businesses with a poor track record of paying back debt on time will be restricted to certain sources, such as mortgages secured on property.

3 a) Debentures and shares:
- Debentures are *loans* from individuals to gain finance **whereas** shares involve giving *ownership* to individuals in return for investment to gain finance.

Hints & tips

Watch for the context in 'Sources of finance' questions. Some answers wouldn't be suitable for **taking over a competitor**, e.g. trade credit or an overdraft. You could also use answers from the 'ways of funding growth' section e.g. divestment.

- Debenture holders receive *interest* payments **whereas** shareholders receive *dividend* payments.

b) Current ratio and acid test ratio:

- Current ratio measures the ability to pay off short-term debts **whereas** the acid test ratio measures the ability to pay off short-term debts in a *crisis situation*.
- The ideal current ratio result is *2:1* **whereas** the acid test ratio result is acceptable at *1:1*.

4 Ways a business can solve cash flow problems:

- Offer cash discounts to customers. **This means** customers are more likely to pay with cash rather than credit which will give more cash to the business.
- Businesses should seek credit from suppliers **which means** they avoid spending their cash reserves and can pay once they have sales revenue.
- Use just-in-time (JIT) inventory control. This involves only ordering inventory when it is needed for production which will improve cash flow **because** it won't tie up money in inventory that is not being used.
- Offer promotions such as Buy One Get One Free (BOGOF) **which will** increase the revenue brought in through sales.
- The business could arrange finance such as an overdraft or bank loan. **This means** it will have the funds available to pay suppliers and avoid running up debts.

5 The role of a manager in the finance department:
Plan – Carry out cash budgets to aid future decision making.
Organise – Arrange for the finance to be in place to give the business funds.
Command – Inform staff of the need to cut costs to improve the financial position.
Co-ordinate – Ensuring staff, e.g. accountants, have support and are on task.
Control – Studying financial statements to control costs, such as expenses.

6 Financial statements a business can use to assess its performance:

- Income statement shows:
  - Gross profit which is the money made from buying and selling inventory.
  - Profit for the year which is the profit made after expenses are deducted.
- Statement of Financial Position shows:
  - The assets the business owns and the liabilities it owns.
  - The total value of what the business owns (Net Assets).

7 Describe the limitations of ratio analysis:

- Ratios don't take internal factors (e.g. staff motivation or staff turnover) into account.

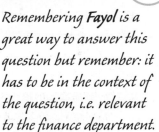

Remember

With 'Explain' questions, give the effect and explain the *cause*, or give the cause and explain the *effect!*

Hints & tips ⭐

Remembering **Fayol** *is a great way to answer this question but remember: it has to be in the context of the question, i.e. relevant to the finance department.*

Hints & tips ⭐

Be sure to read the question; here the most common answer has been excluded in the question wording to make it a bit more difficult.

⇨
- Must compare like for like when comparing with competitors and it is unlikely both firms will be of the same size and type.
- Ratios don't take new product development or recent product launches into account.

8 Gross Profit ratio – ESQ Ltd: 17%, Competition 29%
- ESQ Ltd has a much lower GP percentage than the competition. ESQ Ltd could find a cheaper supplier **which would** lower the cost of sales and therefore improve gross profit.
- They could also look for the marketing department to raise prices **which will** increase revenue generated through sales.

Current ratio – ESQ Ltd: 6.8:1, Competition: 2.3:1
- ESQ Ltd actually has too high a current ratio **because** the ideal ratio is around 2:1 which the competition has so they should look to lower the figure.
- ESQ Ltd may have too many current assets, such as cash which they could invest, for example in developing new products **meaning** the cash could be used to grow the business.

9 'Net assets':
- Net assets is: net assets employed - non-current liabilities.
- It gives the overall value of the business.
- The net assets figure 'matches' the equity figure, i.e. where the amount of net assets came from.

10 Accounting software such as Sage can be used:
- to keep a running total of income from customers.
- to keep track of payments and expenses.
- to send invoices to customers.
- on a smartphone/tablet by employees when out of the office.

Remember

Raising prices or finding a cheaper supplier are the two best ways to increase percentage GP.

Exam-style case study: ASOS

Answers

1 a) Costs of e-commerce/online retailing
- Customers can't try or touch the product before buying.
- Less chance of impulsive buying online than in tangible stores.
- Delivery charges may put some customers off.
- Customers can be wary of entering banking information online.

Benefits of e-commerce/online retailing
- Products can be sold to a worldwide market.
- Products can be sold 24/7, 365 days a year.
- Fewer overheads than 'bricks and mortar' stores, e.g. no rent.
- Online sales expected to rise even further.

b) Process
- Excellent website makes browsing and selecting items easy for customers.
- Image of item on summary reassures customers they have selected right products.

- Size, price and quantity are very clear for customers to see.
- Promotions are visible at checkout, which can encourage sales.
- Secure shopping will make customers feel at ease.
- Wide variety of payment options to allow customers choice.
- Shopping bag visible on 'mini screen' during browsing encourages customers to keep browsing while adding more items.

Hints & tips

*This is a classic Section 1 'lift & add' type of question. You have to take points from the case study/exhibits AND you **must** add to this, in this case with a benefit.*

Product
- ASOS replenishes inventory quickly to reflect current trends, which will appeal to customers looking for the latest fashion.
- Products are worn by celebrities, which will appeal to fans.
- ASOS is launching a range of beauty products which will improve choice for customers.

Promotion
- ASOS uses out-of-the-pipeline promotions such as next-day delivery, which means customers receive their product quickly.
- ASOS has exclusivity agreements which means it offers products that customers can't get elsewhere.
- 'A list' loyalty scheme offers discounts for members, which rewards customers/encourages repeat custom.
- The size suggestion feature reassures customers, encourages orders and reduces the need for returns.
- Student discount makes products more affordable for students.
- Free returns give customers peace of mind.

c) i) ASOS sales revenue is less than that of its rivals because its rivals are more established and have more customers.
- Rivals have more outlets/sell more products.
- M&S has a wider product range (clothing and home) so can meet the needs of more markets.

ASOS sales revenue has been increasing because it has been promoting the business.

Hints & tips

*This is a common 'trends' question. Note the candidate explaining with the word **because**.*

ii) The financial statement that shows sales revenue is an income statement.
- The income statement calculates the gross profit of a business.
- This is calculated by subtracting cost of sales from sales revenue.
- The income statement also calculates profit for the year
- This is calculated by subtracting expenses from gross profit.

d) Functional
Advantages
- Staff can specialise/become experts.
- Staff can seek guidance from others in their field.

Hints & tips

Here the terms you have to discuss are hidden in the case study text rather than asked for in the question. Did you discuss the correct groupings?

Disadvantages
- Slow reactions to external factors.
- Can become more interested in department than organisation.

Location
Advantages
- Staff can meet needs of local market.
- Can react quickly to external factors.

Disadvantages
- Duplication of resources
- Rivalry between location groups

e) Market-led and product-led organisations:
- Product led is when a product is made then marketed to customers; market led is when a product is based on customer wants.
- Product led relies on product development; market led relies on intensive market research.
- Product-led businesses are less responsive to changing external factors; market-led businesses are more responsive to changing external factors.
- Product-led businesses have little competition to begin with; market-led businesses are often in competitive markets.

f) ASOS meets the needs of employees:
- Self esteem/actualisation
  - ASOS promotes internally
  - Career coaching and mentors
  - Job titles such as 'Team Leader'

Hints & tips

Another example of a 'lift & add' question. Here the case study has given the examples and the candidate has matched them up to Maslow's hierarchy.

- Love and belonging
  - Flexible working for employees, e.g. homeworking
  - Holiday allowance

- Additional holidays given for birthdays
  - Team development days such as the Friday 'get-togethers'
- Safety and security
  - Employees receive statutory sick pay when ill
  - Life insurance benefits
- Physiological
  - Good basic pay

g) Decision to manufacture in the UK:
- 'There is manufacturing capacity in the UK' – this gives ASOS a labour market to tap into.
- 'following the pound's decline … domestic production has become more affordable for retailers such as ASOS' – this will save ASOS money compared to producing abroad.
- 'the fashion retailer does teach employees how to stitch and create garments at an academy in one of its London factories' – ASOS is already training UK workers to manufacture clothing.
- 'will be able to serve its European customers faster' – ASOS will be closer to its customers by producing in the UK.

Hints & tips

Again nothing for just 'lifting' - answers from the case study must be added to.

Glossary

Adding value Selling a product for more than it cost to buy

Appraisal A review of an employee's performance

Apprenticeship Paying employees to train while working

Asset Something belonging to a business

Asset lock A way of ensuring that the assets of a social enterprise are used for the benefit of the cause or community

Asset stripping Buying a company intent on selling off all the profitable parts of it

Autocratic leadership Managers are fully in charge of decisions and command employees

Backward vertical integration A business joining with another in an earlier sector of industry in the same market

Board of directors Group who manage a company and make the main decisions

Boston matrix A tool that analyses each part of a product portfolio in terms of market share and market growth

Capital intensive Production using mostly machines

Cash budget Financial statement that looks ahead to the possible cash situation by subtracting future cash outflows from future cash inflows

Centralised management Most control of a business retained at the top

Channel of distribution The chain of businesses or intermediaries that products pass through until they reach the end consumer

Charity A third sector organisation that raises money to benefit others

CMA Competition and Markets Authority is a government department that enforces competition policy to ensure competition and fairness in markets

Conglomerate integration A business joins with a business in a completely different market

Co-operative Democratically owned enterprise that aims to provide a service for its members

Core activities The main tasks of the business, often what it is best at or what is most profitable

Corporate culture The 'feel' of a business, what makes it unique to staff

CSR Corporate Social Responsibility is when companies take responsibility for their effect on the environment or society

Decentralised management Branch or department where managers have most control

Deintegration Selling off part of the business that has been vertically integrated

Delayering Removing a level of management, i.e. *flattening* the structure

Delegation Giving subordinates a chance to do higher-level tasks they wouldn't normally do

De-merger A business splitting into two separate components

Democratic leadership Managers give employees a say in decision-making while remaining in charge

Divestment Selling off an area of the business, e.g. a poorly performing branch

Downsizing Removing staff from the business

Economic cycle   The state of the economy and how, in general, well off customers are

Economic policy   Tools used by the government to help control the economy, i.e. jobs, public funds, inflation, etc.

Employee participation   Getting employees involved in decision-making, e.g. works council

Employee relations   Whether management and employees are on good terms or if there is friction

Empowerment   Giving staff the authority to make their own decisions with some or all aspects of their role

Entrepreneurial structure   Control retained by the owner

Equity   How the business has been funded, e.g. shares

Ethical marketing   Ensuring marketing activities are moral and decent – doing the right thing

Ethical production   Ensuring consideration for the environment and society in the production process

Expenses   Running costs of a business, not including purchasing any assets

Extended marketing mix   People, process and physical evidence are elements of the marketing mix concerning the overall customer experience

External factors   Positive or negative impacts that come from outside the business

External institutions   Third parties that can get involved during a dispute, e.g. trade union or ACAS

Fair trade   Ensuring suppliers receive a decent price for their goods

Fiscal policy   The taxes and public spending part of economic policy

Forward vertical integration   A business joining with another in a later sector of industry in the same market

Franchisee   The owner of an individual branch in a franchise arrangement

Franchiser   The parent company in a franchise arrangement

Franchising   Allowing individuals to own their own branch of a business for a fee and share of profits

Goods   Products that are tangible, i.e. you can physically touch them

Grievance   Concerns or problems that an employee has with their work

Gross profit   Profit made from buying and selling inventory

Herzberg's theory   Theory that two sets of factors motivate or demotivate employees

Horizontal integration   Two businesses from the same sector of industry join together

HMRC   Government department responsible for collecting tax

Income statement   Financial statement that shows gross profit and profit for the year

Internal factors   Positive or negative impacts that come from inside the business

Internal growth   A business growing organically, i.e. naturally, on its own without involving another business (opposite of external growth)

Inventory   Stock of either materials or finished goods

JIT   Just-in-time inventory management ensures inventory only arrives when it is required to make a product

Labour intensive   Production using mostly human workers

Laissez-faire leadership   Managers let employees organise their own tasks and rarely intervene